START AND RUN A

Successful
Complementary
Therapy
Business

START AND RUN A

Successful
Complementary
Therapy
Business

Jackie James

howtobooks / **smallbusinessstart-ups**

Published by How To Books Ltd,
Spring Hill House, Spring Hill Road,
Begbroke, Oxford OX5 1RX, United Kingdom
Tel: (01865) 375794, Fax: (01865) 379162
info@howtobooks.co.uk
www.howtobooks.co.uk

British Library Cataloguing in Publication Data
A catalogue record for this book is available from the British Library

ISBN 978 1 84528 459 6

Produced for How To Books by Deer Park Productions, Tavistock
Typeset by Pantek Arts Ltd, Maidstone, Kent
Printed and bound in Great Britain by Bell & Bain Ltd, Glasgow

CONTENTS

INTRODUCTION

After a successful career in the corporate world, I started my own holistic therapy business. I thought about where my business was going and produced a business and marketing plan. Then I started the work necessary to turn my therapy into a business. I distributed leaflets, gave talks, gave taster treatments, attended health fairs. I put advertisements in newspapers and gradually worked out what worked and what didn't work. With a lot of hard work, I built up a successful therapy business which then evolved into a therapy training company. However, along the way I have wasted a lot of time and money doing things that either didn't work or could have been done better.

I have known many people who have a real gift for their chosen therapy but who have struggled to make their business successful. The truth is that being a great therapist and being a great business person require totally different skills.

The aim of this book is to help you, as a new therapist, to concentrate on doing what you need to do and to stop you wasting time and money by getting it wrong.

This book is split into 12 chapters which cover the following topics:

- ☐ Initially we look at you, your therapies and where to locate your clinic.

- ☐ Then we look at your clients. Who they are, what they have in common and where you can find them.

- ☐ Next we focus on your competitors – not only people who offer the same therapy as you but also other therapists who offer a solution to the same problems as you do. We then look at how to make you stand out and how to influence clients to choose you not your competition.

- ☐ Chapters 5 and 6 look at the different methods of promotion, and help you produce not only your plan for promotion but also your yearly marketing plan.

- ☐ Chapter 7 is all about setting up your business and making the right choices from day one. It starts with choosing a name and helps you to avoid some common mistakes.

- ☐ Chapter 8 looks at the costs of doing business and how to both set your prices and ensure they give you a competitive advantage.

- ☐ The next chapter looks at forecasting and finance. If your chosen business model won't deliver the income you need, find out now so that you can make the changes you need to ensure the business you are building will be profitable and sustainable.

- ☐ Chapter 10 takes you through setting up your business and, importantly, producing your business plan. A business plan is really a description of what you would like your business to look like, and how you are going to make it happen.

- ☐ We then have your business action plan which helps you to prioritize the multitude of tasks you will need to carry out.

- ☐ And finally, you now have all the information you need so the only thing left to do is start your business!

Throughout each chapter you will find case studies and examples which illustrate the essential points. All the case studies are about people I have known but to protect their privacy, I haven't used any real names. Each chapter also contains questions which will help you build up your own business blueprint. Keep your answers in a safe place as you'll need them in the following chapters. Throughout the book you will also find handy tips to help your business flourish and avoid pitfalls.

Following this book from start to finish should help you build your business on solid foundations. So I would like to wish you good luck on your journey and hope you are able to build a thriving therapy business.

1
ALL ABOUT YOU

This chapter concentrates on you as a therapist, the products or services you are offering, your long-term plans, what hours you want to work and how much you want and need to earn. These are all things that you should be considering before you start your business. Knowing all about yourself, allows you to make the right business decisions and set up your business in the best possible way. The information you collect in this section will be used in Chapter 12 when you produce your business plan, so keep all of your exercise answers in a safe place.

Your therapies

This section looks at the therapies you will be offering. This may seem an unusual first step. After all, you have just completed your complementary therapy course so you will be offering the therapy you have just finished studying. This is true, but you need to be clear about two things. Firstly you need to understand how your therapies compare with those offered by other therapists, and secondly you need to know, or have an idea about, the full range of therapies you will be offering. This information will help you make the right choices when setting up your business.

WHAT IS YOUR MAIN THERAPY AND HOW WELL QUALIFIED ARE YOU?

For many therapies there is a choice of qualifications, some being more in-depth than others. For example, to be a reflexologist it is possible to complete a mail order course and never meet your tutor or have had your practical ability assessed. Alternatively, you could have completed an in-depth 12-month course and had your practical ability honed during every single lesson.

Exercise

Write down your main therapy and your qualification. Think about how your qualification relates to other qualifications gained from other courses you could have chosen.

My main therapy is:

....

My main therapy qualification is:

....

Other qualifications available for my main therapy are:

....

How is my qualification better than the alternatives?

....

How is my qualification not as good as the alternatives?

....

....

OTHER QUALIFICATIONS

If you have other qualifications, not related to your therapy, but which show you have achieved a specific standard or have an understanding of health, you might like to use these qualifications. For example, if you have a degree or a nursing qualification, this will reassure prospective clients that you will be a good therapist.

Exercise

Write down any additional qualifications you possess.

....

....

PROFESSIONAL MEMBERSHIPS

You may be a member of a professional organization such as the Federation of Holistic Therapists or the Complementary Therapists Association. You may also be a member of an organization specific to your therapy, such as the Chartered Society of Physiotherapy or the Association of Reflexologists. These memberships are generally valuable indications to the general public of the quality of your work, many ensuring that you are qualified to a good standard and insured.

Exercise

Write down all the organizations you are a member of.

I am a member of the following organizations:

....

I may consider joining the following organizations:

....

....

HAVE YOU SPECIALIZED?

Have you specialized in any particular areas of your therapy? Is there a specific type of person or a particular ailment that interests you? For example, are you a physiotherapist with a particular interest in sports injuries? Are you a homeopath who particularly wants to work with children? Are you a reflexologist who wants to work with the elderly? Are you an acupuncturist who wants to work with clients suffering from infertility?

If you have specialized, how have you gained the additional skills you need in this area? Have you taken additional training courses, is this is an area in which you have lots of experience or do you have any life experiences which help you in your chosen specialism?

Exercise

If you have specialized or you are thinking of specializing, please write it down.

I currently specialize in:

....

I have gained additional skills in this area from:

....

As a therapist I am interested in specializing in:

....

I plan to do the following to increase my knowledge in this area:

....

....

WHAT DO YOU WANT TO ACHIEVE WITH YOUR TREATMENTS?

Sometimes there are no options with this. If you are offering acupuncture, you are looking at helping the client with a specific condition so you are concentrating on their health. But there are a whole range of therapies such as reflexology, aromatherapy, reiki and shiatsu massage where you can change the focus of your treatments and either concentrate on offering a relaxing or pampering treatment, or a treatment focused on making a specific improvement to a client's health.

Exercise

If you are offering a treatment where you have a choice over what you want to achieve, what is it that you want? Are you looking to pamper your clients or do you want to make a difference to their health? Doing one does not exclude the other, but it is important to find out where your interest lies.

The focus of my treatment is:

....

....

WILL YOU BE OFFERING OTHER THERAPIES?

Many people start out with one therapy but find they have very quickly become interested in another therapy and sign up for a course. Or you could already be offering several different therapies, which can affect everything from the name you choose for your business to the type of premises you decide to work in.

Some therapies work together really well, other therapies are very closely related. For example, many hypnotherapists also practise NLP (neuro-linguistic programming) and use both therapies together to achieve results with their clients.

‘ *When Jane set up her reflexology practice she very quickly built up enough regular clients to pay her bills. However, when January came she found her clients suddenly dropped off. As credit card bills became due, clients either cancelled or waited a couple more weeks for their appointment. Jane solved this problem by adding a second therapy to her practice, which was Indian Head Massage. This treatment took just half the time of her reflexology treatments, so she was able to price the treatment at just over half the amount she was charging for reflexology. This brought it into the range that many people were prepared to pay for a Christmas or birthday present. Jane found that she could sell lots of vouchers before Christmas. Her income was still down during January, but she was busy with her voucher clients and she did receive the money when she really needed it, before Christmas.* ’

So think about what therapies you intend to offer, even if your second or third therapies will be some way down the line. It will help you make the right decisions on how to set up your business.

Exercise

If you are going to offer several therapies, either now or in the future, list them here:

....

My qualifications in each of these therapies are:

....

....

 Search the Internet and find registers of practitioners, such as the Federation of Holistic Therapists at http://www.fht.org.uk. Search for therapists offering the same therapy as you and look at what other therapies they are offering. If lots of therapists are offering the same group of therapies, it might give you an indication that they work well together or complement each other in some way.

DO YOU HAVE OTHER SKILLS?

Do you have skills not directly related to your therapies, but which can make you more attractive as a therapist? When a client is suffering from a complex medical condition, for instance, they may be reassured to know that their therapist has additional experience or medical knowledge. However, many qualifications not at all related to your therapy can help. For example, if you have a BSc or a BA it doesn't matter that your qualification is nothing to do with your therapy. It shows that you are able to study and achieve results, and that is important for some potential clients.

> *Jenny is a qualified McTimoney chiropractor who also offers Swedish massage and hot stone therapy. Because her McTimoney qualification is at a higher level than her Swedish massage certificate, having taken her five years to achieve, she attracts more clients with structural health problems than she would if she was only offering Swedish massage. Clients sometimes worry that a massage may make their condition worse, but with Jenny they don't have that concern because of her chiropractic qualification.*

Some therapists have life experiences which can be helpful to clients, especially if the experience is combined with a specialist area. For example, a reflexologist who has experience of infertility may find it easier to empathize with clients who are failing to conceive.

Exercise

Write down any skills or life experiences you have that will add to your therapy.

....

....

 When looking at what skills you have that would enhance your value as a therapist it is very easy to overlook abilities that are obvious to others but which you take for granted. Ask 10 friends to give you five ways you would make a great therapist.

Are you going to sell merchandise?

When you think of therapists supplementing their income by selling products, your first thought might be that this is only applicable to beauty therapists selling very expensive branded beauty products, but this is not the only option.

- As an aromatherapist, you might consider producing your own line of aromatherapy products. Hand creams, body lotions, bath oils and soaps can all be considered, especially if they also possess qualities that distinguish them from mainstream products, such as those that are paraben free.

  Note: Parabens are chemicals that are added to many of the products we buy as preservatives. Many people feel that these added chemicals are not good for our health and can cause us problems. Some people go as far as to say that parabens can cause cancer. If this is an issue you are concerned about, you can help your clients to become aware of the problem and, as a consequence, they may be more willing to purchase your product.

EXAMPLES OF SUPPLEMENTARY PRODUCTS YOU COULD SELL

- As a nutritionalist, you might consider selling supplements, nutritionally balanced products or, depending on your client base, products created for people with specific problems. Gluten-free products are now widely available in supermarkets so would not make a great product to sell, but as other products are produced there is an opportunity for therapists to sell them before they become readily available.

- As a hypnotherapist, you might have your own range of CDs covering everything from giving up smoking to losing weight.

- As a physiotherapist, you may start selling back rests and hand braces.

- As a yoga teacher, you might produce your own meditation CD with a booklet detailing the most common yoga positions you use. This can be sold to your students so that when they practise at home they can be sure they are doing the positions correctly. Almost every home now has a computer with a standard word processing package that gives you almost as many facilities as desktop publishing packages gave you just a few years ago. Producing your booklets is not necessarily easy, but should not give you lots of technical problems. As a yoga teacher, if you have sufficient students, you might also like to consider selling yoga mats and exercise clothes.

□ As a diet consultant there are many diet products on the market that you can choose from.

□ As a reflexologist, you might consider selling your own foot charts, so that clients can find reflexes on their own hands and feet, or selling products to moisturize feet.

□ As an osteopath or chiropractor you may be treating many people who have problems with their backs. This would give you an ideal opportunity to sell products which help either with spinal problems or to alleviate symptoms. For example, you could start with back supports and braces, and move on to products which can be used in the car or at the office.

□ As a beauty therapist you will have specialist knowledge about the type of skin your clients have and the best products for them to use. I'm not aware of any research but I'm sure lots of people start using a face cream in their late teens and are still using the same product into their 40s. During this time their skin condition will have changed dramatically and their original choice of cream may now be totally inappropriate. As a beauty therapist you will have specialist knowledge that could dramatically improve the condition of your client's skin. Choosing the range of products you are going to sell is very important.

Please always remember that when you are selling any product you are selling your reputation. So only sell what you know is a good product.

❛ *Eloise worked for nearly 18 months as a beauty therapist before she found a product range she was happy with. She needed good-quality products, at a price her clients could afford and that gave her the profit margin she needed. But she also wanted a range that was parabens free and broad enough to cover all the skin types of her clients. It was definitely worth the search, because now Eloise has a range she passionately believes is the best available for the price and, because of this, she has no problems selling the products to her clients, especially once they have experienced them first hand when having a facial.* ❜

There are also many products you can sell that are in lots of ways independent of the therapy.

□ A beauty therapist I know sells lovely hand-made jewellery.

□ There are many magnetic products on the market that promise effective relief from back, hip and knee pain. If your client base contains a number

of people with these problems, and you believe in the
products, why not sell them, whatever your therapy?

☐ As a therapist, during treatments I burn high-quality
aromatherapy oils which I sell to my clients. This started
when clients asked me if I could order them a bottle
when I placed my own order with my supplier. Working
this way meant that initially I wasn't investing any money in stock, as
everything I purchased already had a buyer, I didn't have problems storing
a large quantity of oils and there was no chance of them going off.

Sometimes you can sell products which help you to find clients for your own
therapies. For example, there are several large beauty businesses which use
agents to sell their products.

*Laura is a beauty therapist who is also an agent for a well-known large
beauty business. As part of her role Laura has to arrange for people to have
'parties' in their own homes and invite as many of their friends as
possible. Laura carries out a demonstration showing how to use
the products she is selling. So, for example, she may show you how
to change your make-up so that it is on trend for summer, take you
through the correct way of applying eyeliner or carry out a mini-
pedicure to show off the latest nail polish colours. As Laura is a qualified therapist, which she doesn't need to be for her selling role, she is very good
at applying the make-up and carrying out manicure and pedicure treatments.
So, as well as selling products during the 'party', Laura very often finds that
she picks up clients for her own beauty business.*

These are some of the things you need to think about when considering selling any merchandise:

Storage: You will need somewhere to store the items where they will be
             safe and easy to get to. This can be a problem for all products but
             especially for bulky or heavy items.

Safety: If you are storing chemicals, you need to ensure they are not a
             hazard to either yourself, your employees or your family.

Insurance: You need to ensure your products are insured while they are
             being stored.

Spoilage: Merchandise can spoil in several ways:

- ☐ if it has a sell-by or use-by date;

- ☐ if the product manufacturer is likely to bring out a 'newer' model;

- ☐ if the items have to be moved constantly, or have to be stored in a dusty corner, they could lose their 'new look lustre'.

           In any of these cases you need to ensure your turnover is going to be high enough to sell the amount of product you purchase while it is still viable.

Cash flow: For most products you will need to invest money in buying the items before you can sell them and this can have an effect on your cash flow. For some items you may be able to order them directly as you need them but generally you will be able to add in less of a markup than for those products you purchase in bulk.

Returns: If you can get your suppliers to agree to sale or return it can significantly help your cash flow requirements.

Profit: You need to ensure you make enough profit on the items you sell. When looking at the price you pay don't forget to add in all of your other costs, for example, postage if the goods are delivered to you; petrol and running costs of your vehicle if you collect; storage costs; the cost of demonstration products; spoilage costs, for any product that may go off; and other costs such as VAT or other taxes.

You do have to be careful when deciding to sell products. Anything you sell should be chosen carefully so that it adds to your reputation. If you sell a hand cream that separates during storage, or a shiatsu massage cushion which breaks after the first month, you will lose clients. You also have to ensure that your clients do not feel pressurized into buying product from you because, again, it may put them off visiting you at all. I'm sure that, like me, you have been to a spa, received a lovely facial and then felt the experience was tainted because of the high-pressure sales technique of the therapist trying to get you to buy a product that you really didn't want or need.

The best products to sell are those where the client perceives that the product is adding to the treatment, or where the product is just something the client wants to buy.

☐ A physiotherapist who is able to sell their client a knee brace is helping the client. Firstly, by buying from the physiotherapist the client is assured of the quality of the product and, secondly, because the physiotherapist, having examined and treated the client, has very good knowledge about the actual injury or problem, the brace is much more likely to help with the problem.

☐ When I sell essential oils to my clients they are buying them, for the most part, cheaper than they could buy the oils themselves, even from my supplier. Buying direct my clients would pay full price for the product plus postage costs. I get a discount as a therapist and because of the quantity I order I don't pay postage. My clients get good-quality oils and I make a small profit. It certainly isn't a big earner for me but the amount I make is gained with very little effort.

Mandy is a beauty therapist who sells hand-made jewellery. She displays the pieces in her waiting room. The client is always left alone with the products (which are under glass, ensuring there is no problem with theft) so always has an opportunity to look at them. Mandy never tries to sell the jewellery but it is there almost as a service. If a client comes for a makeover before a big event, they may find a piece which complements their outfit. Many of Mandy's clients pick up small items for birthday or Christmas presents, again providing a service because the client then doesn't need to travel into town.

Exercise

Looking at your therapy, can you identify any opportunities to enhance your income by selling particular products? If this is an option, is it something you would like to look at, and how much profit could this make you?

I could sell:

....

The items sell for the following amount:

....

The profit on each item would be:

....

I estimate I could sell this many items each year:

....

This would give me this amount of profit each year:

....

....

What you sell must be commercially viable but doesn't need to make you a great deal of profit. If you can sell a lot of the product, a small amount of profit will soon build up. You may also decide to sell things that will enhance your relationship with your client but, again, you can only do this if you make a profit.

What hours do you want to work?

Are you looking to work full-time, weekdays from 9 a.m. to 5 p.m., or are you looking to work in the evenings to fit in with your family commitments? Are you prepared to work at weekends or are these precious to you for other activities? Do you have any limitations on when you can work, such as not being available during school holidays?

Now think about when you would be willing to work. When we look at your clients in the next chapter there may be some time slots you can offer to your clients which will set you apart from your competition. For example, a physiotherapist may be able to offer early appointments so that clients can visit him or her before they go to work. An aromatherapist might offer late appointments so that the client can go home after the treatment and fall straight asleep! A massage therapist might offer a Saturday morning treatment so that their clients can have a treatment and not have to go to work afterwards.

Exercise

Write down when you would like to work, but also add in when you would be willing to work. For example, you may prefer to work 9 a.m. until 4 p.m. during the week, but might be willing to work Saturday mornings initially to build up your client base. Consider also whether there are any limitations on when you work. For example, if you can only work in the evenings during school holidays.

I would like to work the following days each week:

....

I would like to work the following times during the day:

....

I would be willing to work:

....

I cannot work:

....

....

How much do you need to earn?

This is an important issue, but one that can be forgotten in the rush to start practising.

It can be tempting to look at the hourly rate of your new profession and think that because it is more than your current hourly rate you will have enough money. However, you need to remember that if you are an employee you will be guaranteed payment for all the hours you work in a week. If you are working 37 hours a week, that is what you will be paid for. You will also be paid for holidays, bank holidays and may be paid when you are sick. As a therapist you might find that your work is seasonal. Many therapists offering relaxing therapies find that business is quiet before and after Christmas, while a beauty therapist may be very busy before Christmas, but have almost no clients come the New Year.

So, it is important to work out how much you will need to earn over the year – and, during those months when you earn more, do not be tempted to spend it all.

You also need to take into account:

£

☐ Tax and National Insurance;

☐ If you are registered for VAT you will need to charge VAT on all the services and products you offer. However, this money must be paid regularly to the VAT man;

☐ Rent and other expenses associated with your treatment room;

☐ Expenses, including insurance, membership of your organization and accountancy fees, not just your day-to-day expenses;

☐ You may wish to buy an insurance policy which will pay out should you be unable to work. A word of warning here: if you decide to take out this type of insurance do make sure you are completely covered for what you need. Take care to read the small print. Alternatively you can put aside a specific sum of money each month especially for this purpose, which should only be used if you are ill and unable to work;

☐ You may also decide to put aside an additional amount each month in the event of an unexpected downturn in your client numbers.

Example

If you need to earn £600 each week before tax, you should allow for at least four weeks' holiday a year and not working on bank holidays. This means you will have a maximum of 47 weeks a year to earn your money.

52 weeks, less four weeks' holiday, less one week to account for bank holidays equals 47 weeks.

So the equation is £600 × 52/47 = £664.

This amount does *not* include expenses, or money which needs to be set aside, so to achieve £664 profit each week, you might need to be taking £900 or more in income from treatments. Later in this book we will look at your costs and you will get a better idea of how much income you need to generate before you earn enough money.

Therapists who start in their new profession often don't make enough money to cover their costs in the first few months. If this happens to you, you need to think about how long you can support your business before you start earning the amount of money you need.

Exercise

I would like to earn:

....

I need to earn:

....

I can support myself without income from my therapies for:

....

....

What are your long-term plans?

Think of where you would expect yourself to be in one, five and ten years' time. Will you be doing exactly the same as you are now? For example, you may have spent several years working towards your goal of being a homeopath and, now you are qualified, things couldn't be better. You aim to build up your practice and increase the number of clients you treat, but in ten years' time you intend to be doing exactly what you are doing now, but with more clients.

As a therapist there are other options. You might be thinking that in the future you would like to teach your therapy to new students, either with your own school or with an existing college or university. You might consider starting a clinic, where you, along with other therapists, offer a variety of therapies. You may have always seen yourself writing books. You might want to be involved in carrying out research in your therapy, or your ultimate aim might be to own a spa. Either way, there are lots of options.

If you know where you want to go with your therapies, it can help you make the best choices when setting up your business, in terms of, for example, business name and choice of business model.

Exercise

Think of yourself in one, five and ten years' time and write down how you see your business developing. At this stage you don't have to have all the answers, but if you have ideas now, use them.

Where will I be in	Work location	No. of clients per week	Income	Description of my business
12 months				
5 years				
10 years				

2
LOCATION

Where you work from is important for both your-self and your clients. If you can offer your therapy in a location that is pleasant and relaxing, easier to get to, or which has more abundant parking than your competition, you will have an advantage or may be able to charge a higher price.

Wherever you work you should ensure that your location:

☐ is clean and hygienic – there is nothing so off-putting as a dirty treatment room;

☐ has hand washing facilities either in the room or close by;

☐ has nearby toilet facilities for you and your client;

☐ is safe, for both you and your clients;

☐ is temperature controlled. If you or you clients are too hot or cold, your clients won't get the best from their treatment;

☐ is well ventilated;

☐ is relaxing – even if you are offering a clinical therapy, your client should be able to relax and feel safe in your treatment room;

☐ is professional;

☐ is uncluttered.

Ideally, your treatment room will have a small waiting room, for clients who arrive early, and it is often more convenient to take payment away from the area where you treat. With any treatment room, you are responsible for health and safety and will need to regularly carry out an assessment. This includes your own safety, especially if you are working alone.

❝Betty was a podiatrist who had a home treatment room where she saw her clients. One client, an elderly, almost blind lady of 92, started to give her concerns. A couple of times the client almost tripped when walking up the step to Betty's house. Betty was also concerned that if her children left any toys on the drive and she didn't notice them, her client might fall with disastrous consequences. Betty decided there was nothing she could do to make her home safer, so she started visiting her client in her own home, effectively removing the risk for Betty.❞

You must also ensure that people know where your treatment room is so you will need a sign advertising your business.

There are several different options when considering where you should work, including:

- working at home;

- mobile – working from client's home;

- Using the premises of corporate clients to treat their employees;

- working in a clinic with other therapists;

- renting a room;

- buying or leasing premises;

- running a clinic;

- working at multiple locations.

Working at home

Many people start their new business working from home, which has the advantage that there are minimal costs involved in setting up your room. Ideally you will have a room mostly dedicated to your therapies. However, when you first start this is not always possible and some compromises have to be made. I do know of a therapist who treats in her own lounge. Although she has built up a busy business, she is limited in how much she can charge. It is preferable for your treatment room to be downstairs. I know several therapists who have converted one of their bedrooms to their therapy room and if this is the only option it can be made to work. However, an upstairs treatment room will always put off some clients who will feel uncomfortable going so far into your personal space and some clients who have difficulty using stairs.

‘ *Jasmine is a beauty therapist who offers a range of massage and beauty therapies. She works four full days a week and so decided that it would be worth investing in her business. She converted her garage into a treatment and waiting area where she carries out her consultations, makes appointments and takes payment. She also uses the waiting room to display a selection of beauty products which she sells to her clients. The room has a separate entrance just to the side of her house, allowing her to maintain separation between her family and business. Situated off her waiting room are a downstairs toilet and utility room with hand washing facilities.* ’

If you are considering running your business from home you will need to check the deeds of your house and your house insurance. Although this is not common, some houses have a deed of covenant on them which prohibits any business use of your home.

You will need to inform your insurance company that you are running a business from home and ensure that they will fully cover any claims you need to make.

If you have a large garden, consider having a treatment room built. A variety of timber buildings are now available that are sold as home offices and many of them don't require planning permission. They can have very good insulation and electricity can be installed and water plumbed in. It is more expensive if you need a toilet installed but I know a therapist who has a lovely room in her garden without a toilet. If a client needs to use her facilities, they use her home toilet. Not ideal, but it works for her.

Conservatories can make very good treatment rooms provided there is adequate heating and you have blinds to ensure that clients have privacy and that the conservatory doesn't get too hot in summer.

Most home treatment rooms don't have a waiting room, which gives you the problem of scheduling clients. If you work in a clinic, the client goes to a central reception area to wait until you are available, and to pay and rebook. At your home treatment room a client arriving early can disrupt the client you are currently seeing. If you will be working on your own you need to factor this in, either with a slightly shorter treatment time or a gap between clients.

I allow 15 minutes between appointments. This covers me if I am running slightly late, enables me to give a full treatment if the client is a few minutes late, and allows me to take payment and rebook without giving the client a shorter treatment. Clients know that I have this buffer and if they are early for their appointment they will generally wait in their car until they see the previous client leave.

WHO MUST I INFORM?

If you are going to use a room in your home as a treatment room you will need to contact your local planning department to ensure they are happy with you using part of your home as a business. They are normally concerned with the number of clients you will have visiting you, in case this could cause a disruption to your neighbours. They will need to know if there are adequate parking facilities and they may also ask if your clients will have access to toilet and hand washing facilities. Planning may also restrict any signs you put up advertising your business.

If you have a home treatment room you may be liable for business rates. You are more likely to have to pay business rates if a room is used exclusively as your treatment room, or if the room has been modified to allow it to fulfil its purpose. More information can be found at http://www.2010.voa.gov.uk/rli/ but as each case is considered individually it is imperative that you discuss this with your local council before you start preparing your treatment room.

Although planning and business rates may sound scary, please do contact your local council who are normally very helpful. Many therapists don't have to pay business rates or require planning, especially where they ensure their treatment rooms are dual use, not dedicated as a treatment room.

If you find you do require planning permission and you do have to pay business rates you are more likely to have to pay capital gains on the portion of your home used for business. Again, please ensure you take advice on this matter before proceeding.

Another very important thing you need to do before deciding to work at home is to talk to everyone you live with and make sure they support you, because your decision will affect them. Unless you are very lucky and your room is separate from the rest of the house, anyone else living with you will need to be careful that they don't make too much noise when you have a client. As well as keeping your treatment room clean and tidy, you will also need to keep the entrance to your home clear and the toilet clean. This is not always easy if you have small children or pets. Cooking smells can also put clients  off. If a client enters your home and it smells strongly of, for example, fish or cabbage, they immediately think of your treatment room as less professional.

ADVANTAGES AND DISADVANTAGES

Working from home does allow you to use your time effectively. Especially when you first start and you have long gaps between clients, you can use the time to work on your accounts, do some marketing or even put the washing on.

Advantages	Disadvantages
☐ You can set up your treatment room with very little investment	☐ You may need planning permission, be liable for business rates and for capital gains when you sell. Make sure you check this out before you start
☐ Your home is secure	
☐ No travelling time	
☐ Your equipment is always ready or can be prepared very quickly	☐ Home/work separation can be a problem – you are always at work
☐ You can create your desired environment	☐ Disruption of family – children may need to be kept quiet, pets may need to be kept out of the room
☐ You feel relaxed in your own home	
☐ The room is available whenever you want to work	☐ You can feel isolated
	☐ You or other family members may feel that clients are invading your home
☐ You can use time effectively between clients	
	☐ Limited opportunity to put up advertising signs

TIP If your room is dual use put the equipment you need for your therapy into a pretty box and either store it in a cupboard or display it. When a client is due, everything you need will be in one place and you can get the room ready very quickly.

Being mobile – working from your client's home

Many therapists start off offering a mobile service. This has many advantages. It allows you to treat housebound clients and clients with no transport of their own, or those for whom public transport is too difficult to use. For example, a parent caring for a disabled child might find the bus is just too stressful for her to embark on with her child. For pampering therapies there is also the added advantage that the client can relax in their own home, and for some therapies it is nice for the client to fall asleep straight after their treatment.

There are, however, some disadvantages to working mobile.

- ☐ You will need to ensure that your own transport is suitable. Generally this means using your own car, in which case you will need to check your insurance company covers business usage.

- ☐ Sometimes the equipment you need for your therapy will be bulky or hard to carry. Although portable massage couches are made to be transported, they are not light. They can also be awkward to manoeuvre into small spaces such as a car boot, causing the possibility of strains to backs and arms. This is not something you want at any time but especially if you are a self-employed therapist. Before committing to work as a mobile therapist, you need to ensure you have a safe and easy way of transporting your equipment.

- ☐ Where you use equipment which needs to be sanitized, for example as a podiatrist, you need to ensure you have sufficient sets of equipment to service all of your clients without returning to base to use the autoclave.

- ☐ You need to add in additional time for travelling and loading/unloading your equipment. If you were working in a clinic from 9 a.m. to 5.30 p.m. and had one-hour appointments, you could see seven clients allowing for breaks during the day. If you are mobile, you would be lucky to manage four clients.

☐ The additional cost of travel can be a problem. It's not just the fuel you are paying for. You will have additional wear on your car so you will have additional maintenance costs, you may be paying additional insurance and you may have to pay parking fees. Many mobile therapists charge their clients for mileage, either a fixed rate per mile or they band it, so that for example if the client is within three miles of the therapist they pay £x, if the client is within five miles of the therapist they pay £y.

☐ The environment at the client's house may not be ideal, especially if you are performing a relaxing therapy. The television might be on, the phone might be constantly ringing, their dog might be barking and you might be interrupted during the treatment. The key to getting this right is to agree the ground rules when the client books with you. So you may say you need a private room or, if that is not possible, you need to ensure you are not interrupted. Phones should be switched to the answering machine and other noise kept to a minimum.

☐ If you have a very talkative or lonely client, it can be hard for you to leave. They may keep trying to delay you or make conversation with you. This is difficult because, as a therapist, you can generally empathize with people and want to help. However, if their one-hour appointment takes you two-hours, this is not cost-effective for you and so it is not sustainable. Always ensure your client knows you have to leave on time to get to your next client.

❛ When I changed my own car, just after starting my reflexology course, I visited all the motor dealers in the area with my reflexology couch. Each model I was considering had to pass the reflexology couch test. If the couch didn't fit in the boot of the car, I didn't consider buying it. **❜**

When you first start work as a therapist and don't have a full appointment book it can be tempting to spend longer on your treatments or linger for a while chatting to your clients after their treatment is complete. This is very dangerous because the clients will expect their additional treatment time and come to rely on the time you spend chatting. If you later limit them to the time they have paid for, they will feel the quality of the treatment has been reduced.

☐ Working as a mobile therapist can be very isolating. Although you see your clients and talk about their problems it can get quite lonely, especially if you have been used to working with lots of other people.

☐ Security is always an issue for any therapist, but as a mobile therapist you need to be especially careful. I know of many therapists who have developed lots of different methods to keep themselves safe.

 ☐ Some therapists only accept bookings from people they know or people who are referred to them by somebody they know.

 ☐ Always ensure somebody knows where you are going and when you will be back.

 ☐ Ensure your client knows you are expected 'somewhere' after their session and will be missed if you don't turn up.

 ☐ Call a 'buddy' when you are outside the client's door and ensure the client knows you are making your 'security' call.

 ☐ If you don't know an area, always check it out before visiting a client. If you find the area makes you uncomfortable, you can always cancel the booking.

 ☐ Make sure you have a landline number for the client and call them on the landline before the visit to confirm some detail. You are actually confirming they have given you valid contact information rather than anything else.

 ☐ For a first visit, until you have started to get to know the client, you might consider getting a friend to drop you off at the appointment and pick you up later.

☐ Ensure you check in advance with the client about parking; if you unexpectedly have to pay for your parking or must park too far away from their house it can significantly increase both your costs and the time it takes you to complete the appointment.

☐ As a mobile therapist you cannot display a sign outside your treatment room but you can ensure your therapist's uniform is noticeable and you can attach a magnetic sign to your car. These are available cheaply from many suppliers including www.vistaprint.co.uk.

> *Judie is a massage therapist offering home treatment. When she first started her business she would arrive with her massage couch, four pillows, at least three towels, blanket, box of oils, CD player plus paperwork. Carrying everything inside would take several journeys to and from her car. This was fine if she could park on the client's drive, but sometimes she would be parked some way down the street and when her hands were full of equipment it was difficult to lock her car. She found this really added to the time it took to complete her treatment.*
>
> *Judie decided that this was only going to work if she could transport her equipment in one trip from the car to the client's house. Initially Judie had charged for all travel. She decided to change her pricing structure and not charge for travel within three miles of her home, but to ask the client to provide pillows, towels, a blanket, a CD player if they wanted music and an oil burner if they wanted aromatherapy oils. This meant that Judie could easily transport her equipment in one trip and the extra money she earned by having more time available made up for the amount she lost not charging for travel.*

Using the premises of corporate clients to treat their employees

Many companies are happy to provide a small area for therapists to come in and provide treatments to their staff. As a therapist you need to ensure you know what space has been allocated to you before you arrive to carry out your treatments and that it is suitable. It needs to be fairly private, with interruptions kept to a minimum, so an office with a door is the best option and, if you have a 'No Entry' sign on the door while you are treating, so much the better. Phones can be a nuisance in an office environment, but I have found that as long as the phones aren't within a couple of metres of you, the client is able to zone out.

Ideally, the company would provide the space and pay for the treatment, but this rarely happens. Staff are generally expected to pay for their own treatments, which gives you as a therapist two problems. The first is booking in clients. Some companies do have a reception facility that will take bookings for you, but in most cases staff will need to telephone you directly to arrange their treatment. When you first start you may find you have gaps in your appointment schedule. To encourage more clients, position a whiteboard outside your room/space with a marker pen (attached to it with string or a client will accidentally walk away with it). Draw up a table like the one illustrated. If you have a gap in your schedule and somebody is interested in it, they can write their name and contact number in the space. You can then call them once you have finished your current client to confirm their appointment.

Time	Name	Contact Number
11.30		
12.00		
12.30		

MARKETING YOUR SERVICES

One way of doing this is to site your treatment space in full view of the office. If people can see what you are doing they are more likely to book a treatment themselves, although there is a danger of compromising clients' privacy. This is a fine line which you need to tread carefully.

During the first few times you visit a business, it is worth ensuring you have some clients, even if they aren't paying you. Although 'free' treatments should be avoided, I would recommend giving a manager at the company several vouchers for treatments which they can give to employees as 'rewards'. That way the person receiving the treatment is not getting it free, they have earned it. Alternatively, you could have a competition or prize draw where the winners receive free treatments.

When clients have been to see you once, you must ensure you book them in for their next treatment. One thing to remember with treatments at clients' and premises is that generally people will be able to come for a treatment during their lunch hour. This means your busiest hours at the company are generally between 11.30 a.m. and 2.30 p.m. and, to ensure clients also have time to eat, treatments should be limited to 30 minutes. With such a short treatment time you don't want to be wasting too much time on administration, so make sure clients come to you prepared with a completed medical questionnaire. You need then only confirm details with them rather than take a full history yourself. See Additional Information Sheet 4 at the end of the book for a basic form.

Working in a clinic with other therapists

Working in a clinic as a self-employed therapist can be a great way to start building up your client base because you can leave it to the clinic to arrange your clients; you just turn up ready to work.

ADVANTAGES

☐ The clinic will arrange clients for you.

☐ Reception will normally be provided and you won't need to take clients' money yourself.

☐ The clinic will be responsible for marketing, although you may be asked to help out at any events they run.

☐ Working in a clinic provides a separation from home.

☐ You won't be charged for the room if you have no clients.

☐ Although you will need to tidy the room when you leave, you won't have to clean it or incur any utility or maintenance costs.

☐ There will be other therapists working at the clinic and this can help with the isolation a self-employed therapist can sometimes feel. Some clinics have a coffee area for staff, which is a good way to meet them, or hold regular activities. Otherwise it is possible to work at a clinic for several months and not meet all of the other therapists – if you only work on a Monday you will only meet other Monday therapists.

☐ It is also possible to pick up referrals from other therapists, although you may need to encourage this by offering other practitioners a taster treatment of your own. Once they have experienced your therapy they are much more likely to refer their clients to you.

> *I used to work in a clinic where I treated one of the other therapists each month. She totally bought into my therapy and used to refer clients regularly. However, once she left the clinic I found it very difficult to persuade the other therapists to refer clients to me. Even though I offered them each a treatment, most of them didn't take me up on my offer. Some therapists are never going to refer clients to you but if you find therapists who will, it can be advantageous to both of you.*

DISADVANTAGES

☐ The clinic owner will take a hefty percentage of the amount paid for each treatment, some clinics taking over 50%. However, when you look at the costs involved with running a clinic, such as rent, business rates, reception cover, administration, the cost of using credit cards, cleaning of rooms, marketing and VAT, 50% may seem more acceptable.

☐ You are often not paid for your work until the end of the month.

☐ You normally have to submit an invoice for the work you have completed, which is an additional administrative task.

☐ It isn't always easy to create your own environment. You are using a shared room and, especially if you are sharing with different types of therapist who all have different requirements, the room might not be ideal for you. For example, it may be very clinical or may be focused on relaxation.

☐ There are good and bad therapists you might have to follow. If you follow a Chinese acupuncturist who likes to burn herbs, you may need some time to dissipate the smell!

☐ You may still have to bring equipment with you as if you were mobile.

☐ There can be problems with other therapists running late, which in turn makes you late for your clients. You should ensure there is a buffer built into the room schedule because, even if the previous therapist is on time, they will have to clear away their own equipment and you will need time to set up yours before your first client arrives.

☐ You will incur travelling costs to the venue.

☐ If the clinic successfully fills their rooms with therapists, it may be difficult to increase your hours as you gain more clients.

Renting a room

Renting a room gives you flexibility because you can either rent the room permanently, in which case you can set it up exactly as you want it, or you can rent it for a set period each week, in which case you will be sharing it with other therapists.

Your room should be large enough to hold all your equipment comfortably and if you are only renting it part-time, it helps if there is secure storage for anything you need to leave in the room. Ideally your room should have hand washing facilities within the room.

> *Tracey is an aromatherapist working full-time in a single room in a larger building full of other therapists offering different therapies. Tracey was generally pleased with her room but was very annoyed that clients kept stealing her towels although she was unable to identify exactly who was taking them. When a slightly smaller room became available to rent, Tracey moved rooms. Although the room was smaller it had a sink and water available for Tracey to wash her hands without leaving the room. As well as paying slightly less in rent, Tracey was very pleased to find that, as she remained in the room during the whole time the client was in the room, clients stopped stealing her towels!*

The location of the room is very important. If your room is in a run-down area, people will be loath to visit you. Ideally you want to be somewhere you will pick up passing trade, so signage is very important. If people don't know you are there, you have no hope of them becoming your clients.

> *This case study is about a photographer, not a therapist, but it illustrates the importance of signage. Craig has a studio in a lovely old mill at the edge of a village. The mill is home to over 20 small businesses and so does attract a lot of trade. Before I contacted Craig I had visited the mill on lots of occasions but hadn't realized he was there. When he was giving me directions to his promises he said that I wouldn't have noticed his door. This seemed strange but I assumed he must have recently moved into the building. During the photo session I chatted to Craig and discovered he had been at the mill for over 18 months. I'm sure he would have picked up more trade if he had just had a sign put up advertising his business.*

> *Helena is a beauty and massage therapist who rented a room in a local hairdresser's premises. The hairdresser is on the first floor and the room was nicely placed, off the main reception area. Helena hoped to gain clients from the hairdresser, and planned to carry out quick taster treatments while clients were sitting under the dryer. Another advantage was that the room was cheap, and Helena only needed to treat one client a day to cover her rent.*

Unfortunately, although Helena marketed her services in the local area, she was not successful. Most days she only just covered the cost of her rent, so she was effectively working for nothing. Fairly soon she was forced to give up her room even though she had spent time and money decorating it.

Two major reasons contributed to the failure of Helena's venture. Firstly, as the room was on the first floor and there was nowhere available for Helena to put up a sign, the only people who knew about her were the hairdresser's clients. The second problem was that the hairdresser's business was at the lowest end of the market. Many of their clients were elderly and had neither the money nor the inclination to spend on relaxation and beauty treatments. Sadly, Helena's venture was doomed before it started.

You also need to think very carefully about the other occupants of the building. You don't want anyone who will detract from your services or is noisy. Ideally you should be looking to pick up clients from the other occupants of the building. I once worked in a room next to a hairdresser's which, on the face of it, seemed a good match. However, each time the hairdressers washed a client's hair, they ran the hot water and the noise of the pump echoed in my room, making it impossible to relax my clients.

Check on the availability of parking. If clients have to pay to park as well as for their treatment, they may be put off and choose a therapist at a location where parking is free. Similarly, think about safety. If the parking is on a very busy street, the client may not be happy leaving their expensive new car there.

If the room is dedicated to you, you need to ensure you know when it will be available. Some rooms will only be available during standard office hours and this can limit your earning potential. Check for weekend availability as well as early mornings and late night. If you are going to be the only person using the building out of hours, you also need to think about your own

security. For example, if you are working in your room with your client, is there security to stop people walking in from the street and disturbing you? If you have a client who starts behaving inappropriately, can you get help?

Depending on your agreement to rent/lease the room, you will probably need insurance cover for your equipment, you may be responsible for cleaning and maintaining the room, you may be liable to pay business rates and you may be responsible for paying utility bills. It is important to check all of these things before signing an agreement. And don't forget, if you are hiring the room you are paying for it for 365 days a year, whether or not you are using it and getting income. When you are doing your figures, as well as looking at your holidays and possible sick days, don't forget to factor in public holidays when the building will be closed.

ADVANTAGES

- ☐ There are no disruptions to home and family, the business is totally separate.

- ☐ The building has a professional image.

- ☐ Working in a building with therapists in other rooms can combat isolation.

- ☐ Other practitioners in the building can refer clients.

- ☐ The higher profile of your room may attract more clients, especially if the room is in a prominent position, such as on the high street.

- ☐ You may be able to charge a higher price than if you were working at home.

DISADVANTAGES

- ☐ The biggest disadvantage is the cost of rent, which you still have to pay even if you have no clients.

- ☐ You have set working hours. Generally you will be limited by the hours the building is open, rather than the hours you would prefer to work.

- ☐ You will incur travelling costs to the venue and you may have to transport towels and other equipment back to your home to be washed.

 Before committing to rent a room, talk to the landlord and see if they would be willing to give you a reduction in the rent for an initial period while you build up your client base.

Buying or leasing premises

Buying premises or signing a long-term lease is a very big step and you need to have carried out research and be sure that there is sufficient demand for your services before committing yourself.

You may also need to think about providing reception cover, employing cleaning staff and subletting your rooms to other practitioners when you are not using them, to maximize your possible revenue.

> ❛ *Terry and Jane are therapists offering different therapies. They decided to work together, found a property they liked, and signed a ten-year lease. This worked well and they built up a successful practice, bringing in other practitioners to cover the hours they didn't want to work. However, looking back, they realized that if they had bought the premises, which would have been possible for just a little more outlay, they would now have a very valuable asset on their hands, instead of a property at the end of its lease with no residual value.* ❜

ADVANTAGES

☐ There are no disruptions to home and family, the business is totally separate.

☐ The building has a professional image.

☐ Subletting rooms can bring in additional revenue.

☐ The higher profile of your premises can attract more clients, especially if the premises are in a prominent position such as on the high street.

☐ You can end up with an asset if you buy the premises.

DISADVANTAGES

☐ The biggest disadvantage is the cost of buying or leasing the premises. Remember you are paying for the premises whether or not you are using them.

☐ Set-up costs can be higher, especially if the premises were originally used for another purpose.

☐ You will have set working hours, with less freedom than if you were working from home.

- ☐ Business rates would be payable.

- ☐ You will incur travelling costs to the venue.

- ☐ You can be liable for capital gains tax when you sell.

- ☐ You will be responsible for cleaning and maintenance.

- ☐ If you need to provide reception cover, you will need space, which may cut down on the therapy space available.

- ☐ You will need secure storage for client notes.

- ☐ You will be responsible for all marketing.

- ☐ You will be responsible for health and safety.

- ☐ You will incur utility costs.

- ☐ If you employ reception staff or cleaners you will need employer's liability insurance.

- ☐ You will need to update your public liability insurance so that the premises are covered at all times. Although each therapist you sublet to should have their own public liability insurance, you are responsible for the premises.

- ☐ This is a riskier business option. If you have purchased the building or signed a 10-year lease, and you don't find as many clients as you expected, or generate enough income, you can find yourself in serious financial trouble.

Running a clinic

If you decide to run a clinic you will spend far more time on clinic work than practising your therapies. But it really depends on what you want to do and where you want to go. Clinics can be dedicated to one therapy, may employ several therapists offering many differing therapies, or can cater for a specific type of problem, for example 'Back Pain Clinics'.

Sometimes you are almost pushed into opening a clinic, as in the case study below, where Sarah found a fantastic location which had lots of potential clients ready and waiting. If Sarah had kept to her initial one room with limited hours, another physiotherapist would have moved in and taken advantage of the clients Sarah would not have been able to manage on her own.

❛Sarah set up a physiotherapy clinic in a tennis club. The club was open from 7 a.m. until 10 p.m., seven days a week, and Sarah saw a business opportunity to offer physiotherapy to clients before they went to work and at the end of the day, so that they didn't miss any working time. When Sarah first started she was working alone and using her room less than 50% of the time it was available. So, although Sarah's clinics were always full and she was working hard, because of the amount she had to pay for the room she made little profit. Very quickly Sarah brought in other physiotherapists to make use of the hours when she couldn't work. Her lease prevented her from subletting but it did allow her to open a clinic. The new physiotherapists worked for Sarah on a self-employed basis and initially booking in of clients and taking payment was carried out by each individual physiotherapist. As business increased Sarah recruited a receptionist and a part-time manager so that she could concentrate on her physiotherapy, rather than the day-to-day mechanics of running a clinic. Sarah marketed her service with local GPs and soon, with the clients she picked up from the club, she had a thriving business using all of the three available rooms at the club.❜

 If you decide to run a clinic but don't want too much time away from your own therapies, you need to employ staff for the day-to-day running of the clinic.

If you are looking at leasing premises one of the first things you need to do is check the rules on subletting so you know what options you have. If you bring in other therapists they can either work for you on a self-employed basis or you can employ them directly.

USING SELF-EMPLOYED THERAPISTS

As long as a therapist is also carrying out work for another clinic or they have their own private clients, it is possible to employ them on a self-employed basis. Money from clients all goes directly to the clinic. At the end of the month each self-employed therapist will invoice you for the hours they have worked, and you pay their invoice. This option is a lower risk for you as the clinic owner because you aren't incurring costs if you don't have clients.

It sounds simple, but you need to be very clear about the rules you will be working to. For example, consider the following:

☐ What percentage of the money from the client goes to the therapist?

☐ Who pays for products used during the treatment? For example, Hopi Ear Candles could cost £8 each. If the treatment costs £30, and the therapist receives £15, after paying for their candles they will only make £7. Not much reward for an hour's work.

☐ If the business is VAT registered, is the percentage the therapist receives inclusive or exclusive of the amount of VAT paid? For example, let's consider a therapist who receives half of the amount a client pays. The business then becomes VAT registered. So if a treatment costs £100 plus £20 VAT (assuming 20% VAT), does the therapist receive £50 or £60? The difference between these two amounts will make a big difference to your profit.

☐ If a client is booked but doesn't turn up, does the therapist get paid? Generally most clinics will have a cancellation policy, whereby if a client cancels within a specific period of time they still have to pay, but it is not always that clear-cut. For example, if the client is ill most clinics won't charge because the clinic wants the client to keep coming back. Some people book in but never come, so their late cancellation charge cannot be taken.

☐ If the client pays by cheque and the cheque bounces, does the therapist still get paid?

☐ If the client pays with a fraudulent credit card and the payment is refused, will the therapist still get paid?

☐ If the client has the treatment but for some reason doesn't pay, does the therapist get paid? Although this should never happen clients may leave the building when the receptionist has just popped away from the desk, or the client may have promised to pay at a later date and reneged on that promise. Recovery of bad debts is a problem for all small businesses and it can take a lot of time and effort. Sometimes it just isn't worth this time and effort for the amount outstanding so the debt simple has to be written off.

☐ If the clinic, as part of a promotion, offers money off a treatment, how is that split between the clinic and the therapist?

Many therapists avoid financial management, so it isn't always that easy to get them to submit their invoices on time. The only way is to make it clear, right from the start, that you only pay once they have given you an invoice. Also, do make sure you check the amount they are claiming each month. I would recommend you work out your own figure, and cross-check before paying. Vouchers for treatments can be another source of problems, as you will see from the case study below.

> ❛ *I once worked at a clinic that ran into problems paying therapists when the client was redeeming a voucher. When the treatment was taken the voucher payment was entered on the system as nil. It was then a manual operation to add the correct amount to the therapist's payment. This worked well until the clinic manager left and their replacement didn't pick up on this and didn't pay the therapists. Unfortunately it wasn't noticed by the therapists either for some time, although it would have been if the clinic had insisted on an invoice before paying them. When, after several months, the mistake was discovered, the clinic had to pay their therapists a significant amount of back pay.* ❜

EMPLOYING THERAPISTS DIRECTLY

If you decide to employ therapists directly, you will be responsible for deducting their tax and National Insurance contributions, and you will need employer's liability insurance. Generally, if you employ therapists they will have a contract with you for regular hours. This means you will need to pay them whether or not they have clients, give them paid holidays, and in some circumstances pay sick pay when they are unable to work because of illness. Because of these benefits therapists employed directly will be paid a much lower hourly rate than those employed on a self-employed basis. However, if there is a good demand for their therapies, this can be more lucrative for you, the clinic owner. Many clinics and spas employ beauty and massage therapists and pay them little more than the national minimum wage.

Employers are bound by the Health and Safety at Work Act 1974. The act can be downloaded in full at www.hse.gov.uk/legislation/hswa.pdf.

CHOOSING A COMPUTER SYSTEM

If you are running a clinic with several rooms and multiple therapists, you are more likely to need a computer system to keep control of your business. When looking at systems consider the following:

Booking appointments	Can the system handle different appointment lengths?
Varying therapists' charges	Can the system handle multiple therapists with different charging rates? For example, physiotherapy sessions with Judy might be charged at £90, physiotherapy sessions with Pete might be charged at £70. Sarah may charge £80 for an initial session when she is working as a homeopath but £32 when she provides Indian head massage.
Varying therapists' percentages	Can the system handle multiple therapists who receive different percentages? For example, Judy might receive 60% of the amount charged on her therapies, whereas Pete might receive 50% of the amount charged on his therapies.
Varying charging rates	Can the system handle different charging rates for therapies? For example, you may charge a standard price for general clients, a different price for each insurance company you deal with (as these rates are often negotiated separately) and a staff discount price. You will also need to be able to apply discounts for promotions.

Example

Sarah and Tim are both physiotherapists. Sarah is more senior to Tim so she charges a higher rate for her treatments. So for a session Sarah may charge £80 and Tim £60. Some insurance companies negotiate with a clinic a standard rate for treatments. For example, a fictional insurance company, Xantia, agrees to pay £50 per treatment, which is less than the normal price. Clinics agree to do this because of the volume of work they can receive from insurance companies. This means that if both Sarah and Tim treat an insurance client from Xantia, their charging rate will be £50, which is less than the normal rate. Also, if the clinic has a policy that staff can receive a treatment at 50% of the normal cost, the computer system needs to be able to deal with this. So, if a staff member had a treatment with Sarah they would pay £40, and if the staff member had a treatment with Tim they would pay £30. The computer system needs to be able to handle all these varying rates.

Allocating rooms	If some therapies can only be carried out in specific rooms, can the system ensure the correct room is allocated to the appointment?
Double bookings	Can the system ensure rooms are not double booked? For example, you may have four therapists available during a day, but only three rooms. Can the system book appointments for all four therapists without double booking any rooms?
Statistics and analysis	Can the system provide you with statistics to help you run your business more effectively? For example, your room utilization is a key statistic: some therapists generate a higher profit because their therapies can be sold for more money. They may therefore be more valuable for you than a therapist who works more often but generates less income per appointment.
Marketing	Can the system allow you to send out letters and emails to specific clients? For example, you might want to select all aromatherapy clients who haven't visited the clinic in the past three months. Or you might want to contact all of Janet's homeopathic clients to tell them she is on six months' maternity leave but that appointments are still available with Jeremy.
Invoicing	Does the system allow you to print off client invoices easily and quickly while the client is waiting?
Fees paid by insurance companies	Can the system deal with clients whose fees are being paid by their health insurance companies, raising the required invoice to the health insurance company each month and ensuring any limit placed on the value of the treatment received by the client is enforced?
Outstanding fees	Can the system produce a list of all unpaid fees?
Reporting	Can you print off reports detailing the activity of each therapist each month to allow their invoice values to be checked?

Financial reports	Can you print off an end-of-the-day report to allow you to balance your cash book? For example, you should have £w in cash, £x in cheques, £y in credit card transactions and £z in insurance direct payments.
Accounts	Can you print off reports to allow your accounts to be reconciled each week, month, quarter and year?
Automation	Can the system automatically text or call clients to remind them of their appointment?
Security	Is the system fully password protected, allowing an audit trail for each user of the system?
Ease of use	Is the system easy to use?
Backup	Does the system have a secure and easy-to-use backup facility?

MARKETING THERAPIES

As the owner of the clinic you are responsible for generating enough clients to keep both yourself and all of your therapists busy. This may mean you are marketing therapies of which you have little experience and marketing will take much more of your time than if you were just working for yourself.

Working at multiple locations

When you are looking at the options for your treatment room you should remember they are not mutually exclusive. If you have a home treatment room, you might still like to offer a mobile service to some clients who find transport difficult. You may also think about working in a clinic on one or two days a week. This can help with the isolation you may experience if you only work at home and can also help you to widen your client base.

Shaun works both from his home treatment room and from a clinic several miles away in a doctor's surgery. Each venue attracts different sorts of client and because the clinic is some way from his home, Shaun attracts clients who wouldn't travel all the way to his home treatment room. Shaun earns less per client when treating at the clinic, but he thinks of these as additional clients which he wouldn't pick up at home, so to him it is worth it.

When you are first building your client base, you may find that you have many appointment slots which aren't taken. If you are working at home, or at a clinic where you work as a self-employed therapist but don't incur any room costs, at least you won't be losing money when you are not working. When you are more established you might consider moving to a more permanent arrangement – hiring, leasing or buying either a room or a whole building permanently. Again this is a good argument for working out where you want to be in the future. Although you may wish to have your own premises in five years' time, while you are building up your client base, you may need to compromise.

3
CLIENTS

Who are your clients?

I have run many 'Creating Clients' courses for therapists, and when I ask students, 'Who are your clients?', or 'Who will be your clients?', most therapists say that everyone could be a client, they would be happy to treat anyone. But, while this might be true, different therapists will cater for different types of clients. And those differences will affect not just the way you market your services, but the price you can charge and even where you practise from.

As a reflexologist, my practice is split 80/20 between women and men, and my age range is generally 30 to 60. However, just because most of my clients fit into this group, it doesn't mean that I don't treat children or that I don't have clients in their 90s. It just means that most of my clients fall into a particular age range and when I come to market my services I will get a better result if I market to the people most likely to book a treatment with me which, for me, is women aged between 30 and 60.

As additional examples, a physiotherapist working in a gym may have a clientele which is 70% male, aged 25 to 55, and treat a high number of sports injuries, but a beauty therapist working in a salon may have close to 100% female clientele with an age range between 20 and 60.

When assessing potential clients, think about their gender, age range, income and any specific conditions or ailments they may have in common. When considering the type of people you would like to be your clients, think about what is happening to the population of this country at the present time. Such as:

- ☐ a growth in the over-50s;

- ☐ a decline in traditional two-parent families;

- ☐ an increase in single-parent households;

- ☐ an increase in intentionally childless women.

If you are targeting an area of the population that is growing, it may be easier to build your business.

Exercise

Make a list of the types of people who are your current clients or, if you have recently qualified, make a list of the types of people who came to you while you were doing your case studies.

This is the number of clients I have (or had during my case studies):

....

These clients are split into:

Gender	Under 18	18 to 60	60 plus
Women			
Men			

Many of my clients have this in common:

....

....

If I were to describe a typical client it would be:

....

....

 When you first start in business it is a good idea to talk to other established therapists about their clients. If you choose somebody who won't be in competition with you they are more likely to be helpful. If your therapy association has meetings it is worth attending just for the information you can get from other therapists.

When do your clients want treatments?

Building up a picture of who your clients are can help you work out what time of day they are likely to want treatments. There are no hard and fast rules for this, but consider the following.

- ☐ If you are planning to treat people working a standard nine-to-five day, then early-morning, late-afternoon or early-evening treatments can be more convenient for them because they don't haave to take time off work.

- ☐ Elderly clients may not like leaving home in the evening so may prefer daytime appointments.

- ☐ Parents of preschool and schoolchildren may prefer appointments during the school day.

- ☐ Stay-at-home mums with small infants may find it more convenient to have a treatment in the evening when their partner or their baby's grandparents are available for babysitting duties.

> ❝ *When I first set up practice as a reflexologist I had some daytime clients, but many of my clients wanted evening appointments. I had to wait until I had put my children to bed before starting work so I offered a 7.30 p.m. appointment which worked very well. However, after a while demand outstripped supply and, in desperation, one day I offered a client a 9 p.m. appointment, never thinking they would take it. They did take it and loved it. They could have their treatment and then go home and straight to bed. I offered this time to other clients and I was soon running a 9 p.m. appointment on all the four evenings I worked.* ❞

Sometimes, even if your client finds attending treatments difficult when you want to work, you can make things easier for them, as the case study shows.

> ❝ *Nicki is a physiotherapist who is particularly interested in pregnancy and runs both pre- and post-natal classes. As most of her potential clients are on maternity leave, Nicki scheduled the classes to run during the day. Although many new mums were interested in attending, Nicki found the uptake for her classes was low. This was because the mums found it very difficult to find somebody to look after their babies during the day. Nicki got around this*

> *problem by having a helper at each of her classes. Mums could bring their babies with them in their car seats and if they started crying the helper would rock them gently. Because the mums and babies were in the same room, the mums could relax and the helper did not need to be CRB checked. This would not work in a class aimed at relaxation, but this class was aimed at restoring those muscles stretched and strained by pregnancy and childbirth, so the occasional crying baby, although not ideal, did not disrupt the class.*

You also need to look at your clients to see if their requirements for treatments are seasonal. For example, many therapists find that business is slow in the summer. However, beauty therapists offering bridal make-up will usually be very busy on Saturday mornings, anyone offering spray tans will be busy before summer, and therapists offering waxing will welcome the summer, when they will be run off their feet.

How far will clients travel to see you?

The distance that clients will travel to see you depends on three things:

1. How common your therapy is. If you are offering a readily available therapy, generally clients will be less likely to travel to visit you. If you are the only therapist offering a particular therapy in your county, clients will travel further to see you.

2. If you have specialized. Clients will often be willing to travel further to see a therapist who has more experience in a particular area or who has completed advanced training in a specific subject.

3. If you have a good reputation. Reputations are not built quickly, but they can be worked on. Take every opportunity to talk about your therapy, not only to individuals and groups. Write articles for local newspapers and magazines. Contact your local radio station and ask to talk about your therapy. Carry out research and have the research published.

> *Ruth is a physiotherapist who specialises in women's health. Although she was already an accomplished therapist, by specializing and gaining a great amount of experience, she built up a thriving practice by word of mouth. However, Ruth was not content with this and went on to take a PhD. She now has such a good reputation that clients are willing to travel from the other side of the country to see her. This is not the case for the average*

physiotherapist but Ruth spent a great deal of time honing her skills, which put her in an almost unique position.

 If clients will only travel a limited distance to visit you, one solution is to have clinics in several different locations on different days of the week.

Exercise

Using a local map, mark the areas you will attract clients from. Consider not only clients coming to you by car, but also those using public transport. If you are near a railway station or on a bus route, a client may be able to reach you more easily than someone who lives closer but doesn't have access to any transport links.

Making sure that your target clients can afford your prices

You need to ask yourself if your chosen client base can afford your treatments. If you are trying to sell to people who cannot afford your services you are not going to be successful. You need to either change the people you are trying to sell to, or change the way you package your product so that you are able to make it more affordable.

Exercise

Describe your target clients.

My Clients

Gender split

....

Age range

....

Family circumstances

....

Locations

....

Conditions

....

What do they have in common?

....

Can they afford my treatments?

....

Do they want or need my treatments?

....

....

❛ *Dave is a sports massage therapist who had built up a thriving practice. However, at one point during the recession he found that he was losing clients and some of his regulars were coming much less frequently, which was having a dramatic effect on his income. When he noticed this he started talking to his clients and found that the issue was cost. An hour's sports massage was just too expensive for most of them. To help them, and to increase his income, Dave altered his product range and introduced a sports massage lasting only 30 minutes, for which he charged just over half the cost of his hour's massage. The new massage is very popular and now accounts for over 50% of Dave's business.* ❜

Finding your clients

When you come to market your services, you will achieve most success by targeting your marketing to the people who are most likely to become your clients. So the trick is identifying what your clients have in common.

If your clients are mainly female:

☐ Check if there is a local Ladies' Circle or Women's Institute near you. The age range within these groups can vary considerably, so it is worth visiting the group or phoning the organizer before you spend too much money on marketing to them. Women's Institutes can be made up of women mostly in their 40s, or mostly in their 80s, it really depends on the group.

☐ Investigate the National Childbirth Trust who have pre- and post-natal meetings and tea groups for expectant and new mums and their babies and toddlers. There may be a local group near to you.

☐ Search for events aimed at women. For example, the 'Race for Life' attracts many women who are not necessarily sporty, but who may be the right demographic for you.

If your prospective clients are concerned with their fitness or likely to be sporty:

☐ Advertise in gyms and health clubs.

☐ Display posters in halls where there are fitness classes.

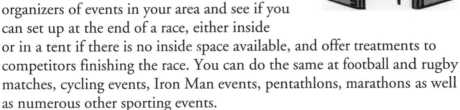

☐ Exhibit or offer short treatments at sporting events. For example, many 10-kilometre races take place around the country. Talk to the organizers of events in your area and see if you can set up at the end of a race, either inside or in a tent if there is no inside space available, and offer treatments to competitors finishing the race. You can do the same at football and rugby matches, cycling events, Iron Man events, pentathlons, marathons as well as numerous other sporting events.

If your clients are likely to be over 50:

☐ Look at the Royal British Legion or the Royal British Legion Women's Section.

☐ Investigate the Phoenix Over 55 Club.

☐ Contact the Probus Club, which is a business and professional club for men aged over 60.

☐ Consider advertising in local Older People's Forum newsletters or arrange to talk about your therapy at one of their open meetings. An older person is classed as somebody over 50.

Also, don't forget you can approach businesses and ask to advertise on their noticeboards or internal Internet sites, school parent–teacher associations, libraries, sports clubs, care homes, clubs such as slimming or needlework clubs, and associations offering information and support for people with medical conditions, such as the MS Society.

You also need to ensure you market in a wide enough area. If your clients will travel 20 miles to see you, you need to be marketing to the whole of your catchment area, which could include several different groups.

Exercise

Think about your prospective client base and make a list of some of the places where you may choose to market to them.

My potential clients can be found:

....

....

4
COMPETITORS

Identifying your competitors

When you are identifying your competitors, start by considering practitioners with the same qualification as you. The easiest way to do this is to use your own therapy organization's list of practitioners. For example, I am a member of the Association of Reflexologists and can search for all reflexologists in my area.

Next, look at people who offer the same therapy as you, but who don't necessarily have the same qualification as you. (For example, you can call yourself a hypnotherapist after completing a mail-order training course, a weekend training course or a comprehensive diploma.) The easiest way to do  this is to use either an online directory such as yell.com and enter your therapy into the search criteria, or a business directory. When you are looking at your competitors, you will know the difference between the various qualifications and the implications for the type of treatment they provide, even though the general public may not have this information.

The next step is to widen your search and look at therapists offering different solutions to the same problems. For example, if somebody has back pain, they may consider visiting a physiotherapist, an osteopath or a chiropractor. Although all three therapies are different, they all offer a possible solution to a person with the same problem. Again I would use an online directory such as yell.com to find these therapists.

Now that you have looked at the 'complementary' alternatives, you need to consider what is available from statutory organizations. For example, physiotherapy is available on the NHS, as is acupuncture.

Exercise

Make a list of your competitors who fall within the catchment area you have identified for your therapy (see the map you marked in the exercise in Chapter 3). Select a variety of competitors and for each one find out:

☐ their price, including what is included in the price;

☐ the length of their treatment;

☐ their location;

☐ their qualifications;

☐ what other therapies they offer;

☐ what other services they offer;

☐ how their service is similar to yours;

☐ how their service is different from yours;

☐ in what way you feel your service is better than theirs;

☐ what aspect of their service, if any, is better than yours.

Analysis for Treatment A			
	Competitor 1	Competitor 2	Competitor 3
Price			
Length of treatment			
Location			
Qualifications			
Other therapies			
Other services			
Similarities			
Differences			
I am better because ...			
They are better because ...			

You will use the information above when you work out how you can stand out from your competition – in other words, what is your competitive advantage – and in helping you to decide what price you should charge for your treatments.

 When you have finished using your research above, put all the information you have collected in a file and place it at the top of your bookcase. This time next year get out your competitor file and see if anything has changed. Check out the people you spoke to last time and search the Internet and *Yellow Pages* to see if you have any new competition. It is really important to check regularly – at least annually – that you are still competitive.

Standing out from the competition

Before booking a treatment any prospective client will generally look at a number of therapists before deciding who they will book with. When you are marketing yourself, your whole aim is to make yourself stand out from the competition so that clients will book with *you*, rather than with your competitors.

Exercise

Think about the last time you chose to visit a new therapist. Did you look at several therapists? What made you decide on your final choice?

Prospective clients will look at a number of factors which may include:

☐ your qualifications;

☐ which professional organizations you belong to;

☐ whether you are dedicated to one particular therapy;

☐ if you offer other therapies;

☐ how long they will need to wait before they can be treated;

☐ whether they can see you at a time which is convenient for them;

☐ whether it is easy for them to get to;

☐ whether your location is pleasant/relaxing/safe.

It can be difficult when you first start to find something that differentiates you but, if you look at the list above, surprisingly, offering several therapies and being dedicated to just one therapy are both selling points, depending on what the client is looking for.

Ali is a holistic therapist who is passionate about ensuring everything she uses is organic, sustainable and, as far as possible, additive free. She even uses natural cleaning products in her house, so she uses this in her marketing to differentiate herself from her competition. Ali is working in a niche market but has made herself much more attractive to people who, like her, are concerned about the possible harmful effects of pesticides and additives.

Exercise

Make a list of the ways in which you stand out from your competition. Include anything about you, your therapies and your location.

....

....

....

....

....

....

5
PROMOTION

In order to become successful as a therapist you will need to work hard to promote your business and build up your clients. Promotion should:

☐ raise awareness of you and your therapies;

☐ encourage people to come to you and try your therapies;

☐ encourage clients to come back for more treatments.

There are many ways to promote your business and in this chapter we will look at the different types of promotion you could use.

Exercise

Look at the six categories of promotion in the diagram below and take three minutes to write down all the different methods of promotion associated with each category.

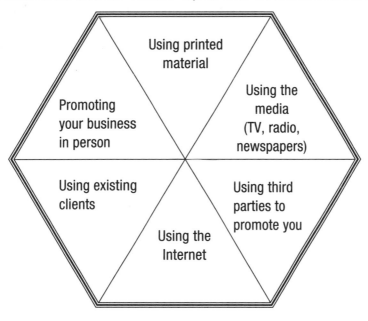

....

....

Exercise

Before you start any sort of promotion, rehearse what you would say to a prospective client if they telephoned you or, better still, ask a friend to call you and ask for details about your therapies. This exercise is much more difficult than you may think it will be.

Using printed material

Generally, printed materials are a cheap method of making sure anyone interested in visiting you for a treatment has your full contact details but they can also be used much more extensively to generate interest in your therapies.

This section will look at the following printed promotional material:

- ☐ Business cards;

- ☐ Posters;

- ☐ Leaflets;

- ☐ Listings directories.

BUSINESS CARDS

These only work if you give them out so always have your business cards on you and if somebody needs your number, for any reason, give them a card. If you need to write something down for anybody, write it on the back of your business card.

Some therapists have the back of their business cards printed so that they can be used for client appointments. That way your clients always have your number if they need to contact you or recommend you.

Make sure your cards are of a reasonable quality. You don't need to spend a fortune, but I would caution against printing your own. There are now several Internet providers who offer good-quality cards cheaply, so don't spend too much money while you are still experimenting with the look and feel you want to go for.

'*As a therapist I originally bought very plain business cards but after a short while I felt they didn't stand out enough. So I went for a card with a picture which showed clearly I was a therapist. I was very pleased with the cards until I discovered that several other therapists were using the same picture. I then went for a bespoke logo which I customized from those available on an Internet site. These are the cards I currently use and I am very happy with them.* '

When you are buying business cards from the Internet, don't go for the most obvious pictures or illustrations because other therapists in your area are probably already using them. However, at the other end of the scale, when you first start don't spend hundreds of pounds on a logo for your business unless you are very sure of the look you are going for and the message you are trying to convey.

POSTERS

Posters can make potential clients notice you. Generally you will be limited to A4 posters (which is the standard size of normal printer paper) as this is the preferred size for noticeboard owners. Anything bigger will not leave enough room for other advertisers. When you are designing your poster, keep it simple. The most common mistake people make is to cram too much information into too small a space. This makes your poster look too busy and nothing stands out. A good picture is worth a great deal of words so, ideally, go for as large a picture as possible, to capture the attention of the viewer. And some very brief details of what you are promoting, with your contact details in a larger type size. If people are interested they can contact you directly for more information.

Initially you can display posters informing potential clients you have just opened in the area, but posters can also be used in other circumstances. For example, if your therapy is a pampering therapy, you can advertise gift vouchers for Mother's Day. If your work is seasonal, you can remind people that it is available now. You should display your posters wherever you can. Try your local library, parish council notice board, GP's surgery, leisure centres, newsagents, the post office; anywhere your potential clients might be.

Have your posters laminated if they are going to be displayed outside or will be displayed for more than one month. This will keep them looking fresh for much longer.

LEAFLETS

If you produce a leaflet advertising your therapy and deliver it to all the houses in your local area it will generate very few telephone calls and even fewer bookings. Many students on my 'Creating Clients' courses have tried this and found it hasn't worked for them. The problem is generally that they are working with numbers which are significantly too small. With any leaflet drop advertising any service, you are doing well if you get even 0.5% of people to call you back. Put another way, if you distribute 100 leaflets, you will be doing really well if you get a response of half a person; not good odds. If you do decide to distribute leaflets, you need to send out at least 1,000, preferably 2,000. Including an offer, for example, £5 off a treatment if you show this leaflet, will normally increase your response rate slightly, and if you do a second leaflet drop a couple of months later, you will get more people remembering you. So the question is, if the response rate is so small, is

it worth it? I would say yes, but you should be looking at this as one of a series of marketing initiatives. If somebody sees your leaflet on their mat and notices your poster in the newsagent's, when they later see you are doing taster treatments at the local school's fundraising pamper evening, your name will already feel familiar to them so they may be more likely to try a treatment. So, do your leaflet drop, but always do it alongside some more targeted promotion.

Designing a leaflet

When a potential client sees your leaflet they are getting their first impression of you, so it is important that your leaflets are professional. Most people try to include too much information and end up with a cluttered leaflet that nobody reads. The quality of paper you use needs careful consideration. Too thin and it will look cheap, too thick and the client may feel you are spending so much on promotion that you will either be very expensive or will cut corners on your treatment to reduce your costs.

You also need to decide if you are going to fold the leaflet. Many therapists print out their leaflet on A4 paper and then fold it into three so that it's not too bulky for prospective clients to keep. This works well as long as the leaflets are folded neatly but if you are folding 1,000 leaflets then the quality of the workmanship may deteriorate as you get tired, especially if family and friends are helping you. If you are going for the three-fold option, you should consider having your leaflets produced professionally. If you are producing your own you may find that using an A5 leaflet (half the size of standard printer paper), unfolded, is less hassle.

Always include the following information in all your leaflets:

☐ Either your own name or your business name and contact details;

☐ The location of your clinic or the area you practise in;

☐ The therapy or therapies you are offering;

☐ The benefits of your therapies;

☐ A sentence or two saying why the potential client should choose you rather than your competition;

☐ A line inviting potential clients to call you so that you can answer any questions or so that they can book an appointment.

You should also consider including some of the following:

☐ An interesting picture or logo to draw the client in;

☐ Your qualifications, including any letters after your name;

☐ An explanation of your therapies;

☐ The prices of your treatments. Some people feel you should not include prices, reasoning that if a prospective client needs to call you to find out about the price, you have an opporunity to convince them of the benefits of booking a treatment with you. The alternative view is that if the price isn't in the leaflet, prospective clients may feel the service will be too expensive so won't even call. I generally don't include prices in my leaflets, but I have an insert which contains the price list. That way I can include it when I see fit.

Exercise

Design a leaflet or poster to promote the therapies and services you offer.

Ask all your friends to collect leaflets from as many therapists as possible, even if they are not offering the same therapies as you. This will give you lots of ideas for your own leaflets. You can see what works and what doesn't. For example, if somebody has used a very thick piece of paper, what does that tell you? You might think that is great, or you may consider that it is a waste of money and that their therapies will probably be more expensive. You can find spelling mistakes on other people's work much more easily than you can on your own. If you find a spelling mistake, how does it make you feel about the therapist? If they are sloppy about their leaflets, are they sloppy with their therapy or their hygiene?

LISTINGS DIRECTORIES

Many local listings directories, such as *Yellow Pages* and *Thomson Local Directories*, allow you a free listing. You should always take advantage of free listings and if you are on the geographical border between two editions you may be able to get an entry in both.

There are circumstances when you might consider upgrading your entry and paying for a larger advertisement. Look at how many other therapists are in your section. If there are just a few others, and your entry is displayed near the top of the printed list, consider how much you would gain from having a larger entry. If there are aspects of your therapy that give you an edge over your competitors, and that you can advertise to potential clients, this may be worth doing. On the other hand, if there are lots of therapists listed in your section and your entry is nowhere near the top of the list, you are likely to benefit from paying for a larger advertisement nearer the top of the list. Most printed listings directories are also available on the Internet so, when you are looking at how your free entry is displayed, you should also check the online version. If you aren't displayed on the first page clients are unlikely to choose you.

' *Wendy and Katy both studied together and set up their businesses at the same time, although they lived about 70 miles away from each other. They carried out an experiment. Wendy had a free one-line entry in the local directory advertising her business. Katy paid for an advertisement with the same company. Although Katy received a discount for booking within the umbrella of her governing body, she still had to carry out almost one treatment a month to cover the cost of the advertisement. For the first year Wendy and Katy each made a note of how many phone calls and clients they gained from their adverts. Although this is a totally unscientific study, and there were probably additional factors which aren't covered here, Wendy actually picked up slightly more clients. If you allow for the fact that Katy had to carry out 12 treatments just to break even, then Wendy seemed to have made the correct decision to stick to her free line.* '

Generally, looking at any publication, advertisements on the right-hand page will be more visible than those on the left-hand side (try this out). Again, the most common mistake people make is to try and cram in too much information in a small space. They also concentrate on things that are irrelevant to clients, such as the company name. The company name needs to be there, but not necessarily in big, bold letters.

Exercise

You are going to put an advertisement in a directory such as *Yellow Pages* or *Thomson Local*. Contact the publication and find out the cost of different-sized advertisements and choose the most appropriate for you. Either on a computer or with paper and pencil, create a mock-up of your advertisement, making sure the paper colour is the same as the publication in which you are advertising. Cut out your advertisment, open your publication at the page your advert would appear on and ask somebody to place your advertisement on the page while you are looking away (a blob of glue will help it stay in place), but ask them not  to go for the centre of the page. Look at your advert. Ask yourself if it stands out. If it doesn't, which adverts do? If necessary, redesign your advertisement until it really makes an impact.

Meeting potential clients in person

The most effective forms of promotion are the ones where you meet and/or treat potential clients. You can do this by having an open day at your therapy room, exhibiting at an exhibition, offering taster treatments, giving a talk or a demonstration of your therapy and, in some very narrow circumstances, giving away a free treatment.

ARRANGING AN OPEN DAY

If you have your own room or even if you are renting a room by the session, have an open day. Invite all of your friends and work colleagues and ask them to bring with them somebody you don't know. Offer them incentives to come on the day, for example, free samples or discount vouchers to be used later. Be wary of giving taster treatments on these days because you need to be available to greet people and tell them about your new business. If you want to offer taster treatments, book them in for an appointment during the following week.

EXHIBITING AT HEALTH EVENTS

Exhibiting at an event is a great way of finding new clients because you can talk to potential clients and start to build up a trust relationship with them.

If you are booking yourself a space at an exhibition, make sure you ask:

- ☐ How will the event be marketed?

- ☐ Which other exhibitors are attending and what therapies are they offering? If most of the exhibitors offer spiritual-based therapies, the fair won't necessarily attract visitors interested in their health.

- ☐ Is there a limit on the number of exhibitors offering the same taster treatment or selling the same product? I have been to fairs where there have been many therapists offering the same therapy, which made it harder for any of them to have a successful event.

- ☐ How much space will you have?

- ☐ How many visitors are they expecting or, if they don't know, has there been a similar event and, if so, how many visitors attended that event?

- ☐ What equipment will be provided? Some events provide tables and chairs, others may not.

- If tables are being provided, how big are they?

- Is there access to a power socket and, if yes, would there be an extra charge for this?

- Is the whole event in one room? When an event uses several rooms, some rooms can be 'dead' rooms as far as visitors are concerned. If there is a choice, you are better off in the biggest room.

- Where in the room will you be placed? Again, some positions are better than others. Generally, people go straight past the exhibitor next to the door because they don't want to cause an obstruction.

 If possible, attend an event from the same organizer before you book your place, to make sure the event is suitable for your therapy.

Having booked your place, the next thing to do is think about what it is you want to achieve from the event. This can be to make money, sell your product, find new clients, build up a contact list of people who might be interested in your business or raise awareness of yourself or your complementary therapies. You then need to decide the best way to allow you to do this. For example, if you are offering taster treatments and your aim is to find new clients, you might want to set the cost of the treatments low to encourage more people to try your treatment. Alternatively, to encourage clients to book with you after the event, you might offer them a refund of the cost of the taster treatment if they book a full treatment with you while they are at the event.

If your aim is to gain names and contact details of people who might be interested in your business, you could consider running a free raffle where visitors have to provide you with their contact details in exchange for the chance to win a prize.

Whatever your aim you will have more success if you increase your interaction with the visitors to the event, so think about how you could do this. Here are some examples:

- Have a quiz and test the visitors' knowledge. You don't even need a prize.

- Freebies are always popular but they need your name and contact details printed on them.

☐ A personal trainer could bring in an exercise cycle and offer fitness assessments, first checking clients' resting heartbeat and then checking it again after exercise.

☐ A nutritionist could bake some tasty but healthy treats and hand them out.

☐ You can give out samples of your product, whether this is hand cream or an energy drink.

☐ An exhibitor selling creams and lotions could offer impromptu hand massage.

☐ You can demonstrate your product:

  ☐ I have seen an exhibitor exfoliate and moisturize a visitor's hand and then let the visitor feel the difference between the treated and the untreated hand.

  ☐ I have seen an exhibitor buff a single nail so that it is smooth and shiny. Again, the contrast between the visitor's untreated nails and the enhanced condition of the treated nail is very important.

☐ An exhibitor selling crystals could have information on the properties of some of the more common types of crystal. For example, moonstone is said to increase intuition. Although the exhibitor knows a lot about their crystals, most visitors will know very little.

☐ A reflexologist could demonstrate some easy reflexes on visitors' hands. For example, the areas beneficial to the uterus and ovaries are easy to find.

☐ A chiropractor or osteopath may offer spinal assessments.

The above examples are to give you ideas and hopefully they will help you think of something innovative for your therapy or health product or service.

It is important to set up your display area so that it looks both professional and inviting. You may be able to bring in a screen to make your area more private; a tablecloth can make your table look more professional, as the tables at these events tend to be functional but lacking in style; and flowers or other display items can help your stand look interesting.

☐ Where possible, put together a display. This can be on your table or on a board which can be displayed near you. Sturdy boards work better than paper and, where possible, laminate.

☐ When you are choosing what to display, try to sell 'solutions to problems' rather than your therapy. You can catch someone's eye by offering them help with their bad back, insomnia, infertility or hay fever, for instance. As a reflexologist I normally choose two or three things to focus on.

☐ It is good to include newspaper articles, especially if they contain links to your chosen area of focus. For example, the acupuncture fertility link must be true if it is printed in a newspaper!

☐ Ensure you have available literature containing your contact details and price list. This seems obvious but I have seen exhibitors arrive at a fair with nothing except themselves.

☐ Don't put too much on your display stand. If the area is too busy visitors won't be able to work out what you are offering.

☐ If you will be working on the stand on your own, think about security, especially for when you need to visit the toilet or grab a hot drink.

☐ Burning aromatherapy essential oils adds to the atmosphere, but please always keep to the list of safe oils. I have been to events where people have burnt oils which are contraindicated during pregnancy, which is not at all professional.

☐ If you are offering Hopi Ear Candles as a treatment, you may like to include a display of some of the more unusual ear candles. I have a set from America which are over a foot long, as well as a tiny pair of candles from Europe.

☐ If you are offering taster treatments you don't need complete privacy. In fact, for you to be most successful, other visitors need to see you carrying out treatments.

Projecting the right image

Your appearance is very important on these occasions. Make sure you look professional and are dressed appropriately. You are selling yourself so your look should reflect your values. If you are a holistic therapist offering healing you may go for a more informal look than if, for example, you are offering clinical acupuncture. I have seen therapists at fairs wearing old jeans and dirty tops and that definitely doesn't give the right impression. You don't have to wear a therapist's tunic, but in my experience the most appropriately dressed exhibitors are definitely busier than those who have not made an effort.

- ☐ Make sure people know your name; badges are good, as are notices on your display area.

- ☐ If you are a member of any professional organizations or are highly qualified, make sure people are aware of this. Again, put this information on your badge or use a poster.

- ☐ Don't spend all your time behind your table/couch. You will be much more approachable if you come out and talk.

- ☐ Don't spend all your time sitting down. If you aren't talking to anyone, you are more approachable if you are standing. I recommend you don't even have a chair to sit on unless you need it to carry out your therapy.

- ☐ Smile – if you are looking grumpy and stressed, you are not a good advertisement for your therapy!

OFFERING TASTER TREATMENTS

Offering taster treatments, whether you are an osteopath or a Bowen practitioner, is a great way to find new clients.

The length of the treatment offered depends to some extent on the treatment you are offering, but if your aim is to find new clients you need to treat as many people as possible during the day. I think a 10- or 12-minute treatment is normally about right. I have tried this for both reflexology and Indian head massage and this timing allows you to treat lots of clients, and gives them a taste of your treatment, but definitely leaves them wanting more, which is so important. If you are offering alternative therapies like ear candles you will be limited because each Hopi candle takes about 10 minutes to burn down, but most holistic therapies give you scope to choose the treatment timing. Whatever you go with, if you are not used to giving taster treatments it is a good idea to have a clock on your table so that you can check if you are keeping to time – and make sure that you have practised beforehand.

When you are setting your price you need to remember that if your aim is to create clients, you need to treat as many people as possible. So you want to set your price low enough not to put people off, but high enough that they value the treatment. So, if I was charging £40 for an hour's aromatherapy treatment, for a 10-minute taster treatment I would charge only £5 to £8.

While we are on the subject of payments, make sure you have somewhere safe to keep your money and ensure you have a float. Your first customer is bound to pay with a £20 note! Also, make sure you have a prominent price list for the treatments you are offering on the day. People won't ask so without one you will lose clients. If there is going to be another therapist offering the same treatment as you, it can be worth producing a couple of different price lists. That way, if you need to reduce or increase your price to remain competitive, you can do this easily and still remain professional. I have seen exhibitors scribble out their prices and write in new ones, which always looks awful.

 When I am giving taster treatments I always offer to refund the cost of the taster treatment against a full treatment as long as the client books with me at the event. So, don't forget to have your diary with you!

Although when you are giving taster treatments you don't need to carry out a full consultation, as the opportunities to tailor your treatment to your client's specific needs will be minimal, as a professional therapist it is always important to ensure the client completes a medical questionnaire and signs to say they are happy to have a treatment. To ensure  this doesn't cost you too much time, have pre-prepared forms for customers to fill in themselves. All you need is their name, address, GP details if appropriate, their contact number and enough medical questions to ensure you can tell if they are contraindicated. A sample form is contained in Additional Information Sheet 4. That way all you have to do is confirm the details with the client and you can start the treatment. Don't forget to take plenty of pens, as a single pen will always get lost, and a board or something similar for the customer to lean on when filling in the form.

 Have preprinted aftercare advice sheets available. This helps you offer aftercare advice quickly, the client will have a written record of it to refer to (even a short treatment can leave clients very relaxed, so that they don't always take in information) and the client takes away something with your name and contact details on it.

One question I am often asked is, 'How do I book in customers when I am busy giving a treatment?' This is important because if you interrupt the client you are treating to talk to somebody else, you risk making them dissatisfied with their treatment. And if you don't book a passing client in for their treatment, they may not come back. To get around this you need a Taster Treatment Booking Form. This gives instructions to visitors to write their name in a timed slot, fill in a medical consultation form and then come back at the allotted time. You leave the forms on your table in plain view, so if you are busy giving a treatment, customers can put their name down for a specific time. An example form can be found in Additional Information Sheet 3 at the end of the book.

Make sure you leave time between your treatments for washing your hands, etc. There are gels on the market that you can use which don't need water but every so often you should still wash your hands with soap and water. You don't need to include a break for your lunch – if you are really busy just put your own name in one of the treatment slots. People like busy forms!

If you offer water after treatments make sure you have some plastic cups and mineral water or a container to collect tap water, which is often available but not always conveniently situated.

Also consider using couch roll; you won't want loads of towels to wash after the fair and probably won't have room to store them anyway. And remember to take a large bin bag with you for your used couch roll and your other waste. You don't want to waste time visiting the bin after each client, and a pile of used couch roll behind your couch looks unhygienic and unprofessional.

TIP *how to books • small business start-ups*

Ask a friend to come and have a treatment early on in the day. People are much more likely to try a treatment if they have seen somebody else have one first, especially if they look *s-o-o-o* relaxed.

GIVING TALKS AND DEMONSTRATIONS

These are also a great way of finding new clients, but giving a talk can seem very daunting. I gave my first talk and demonstration on reflexology just one week after taking my final exams. This gave me several problems. Although

I was fairly sure I had passed my exams, I hadn't yet received my results, which dented my confidence a little. Secondly, with the event coming so soon after my exams, I was left with very little time to prepare. However, the local school's PTA had approached me and I was worried that if I didn't accept, they wouldn't ask again. In lots of ways the experience was really good for me because I had no time to worry and, perhaps because of this, it all went very well and provided me with three clients for my new business.

When you are giving a talk it is important just to be yourself. But there are some rules which will help make the talk more successful. Look back to Chapter 2, and decide if the event will attract the sort of people who are likely to become your clients. For example, if you are giving a talk in a gym frequented by adults and your clients are mostly children, the venue isn't going to be much use to you, so you should consider if it is a worthwhile use of your time.

Knowing your audience is very important. If I am going to talk to an organization who meet regularly, such as the WI, then I will go to one of their meetings and just have a look at the people who are attending. WI groups can encompass a wide age range. They can be full of women of childbearing age, or comprised mainly of women well past the menopause. Either way, you need to know, for two reasons. Firstly, you must ask yourself if these people are likely to become your clients and, secondly, you need to tailor your talk to audience.

Before you begin

- ☐ Find out who are your audience.

- ☐ Decide what message you want to give them – what will make them most likely to book a treatment with you or buy your product. Sometimes, even though your particular therapy is effective in treating a wide range of complaints, it is more useful to focus on a narrower area, such as 'Women's Health', 'Treating Children' or 'Combating Stress'.

- ☐ Decide if you want to give a talk or a demonstration treatment.

- ☐ If you are giving a demonstration treatment work out how to choose your client. Generally you will have many willing volunteers, and you want to appear fair when making your choice. If you are nervous I would suggest you approach somebody before your presentation starts. If you are more confident you can ask for a show of hands and then make your choice.

‘ *When carrying out a demonstration during a talk I once asked people to put their names into a hat before the event. My thinking was that I could use their contact information to market to them after the event. I chose a client randomly but this method didn't work as well as I had anticipated. I found my random client was an elderly lady who was well over the 17-stone weight limit of my couch. Unable to let her sit on my recliner put me in a very awkward position. I couldn't say, 'Sorry, I can't treat you as you are too fat' in front of the rest of the audience so, for what seemed an eternity, but I'm sure was just a couple of seconds, I stood there and tried to find a way out of my predicament. Luckily, I was doing a reflexology demonstration, and clients can be given treatments on their feet or their hands. I decided to change my game plan and I gave her a hand treatment which allowed her to sit in a normal chair. It all worked out well but it isn't a situation I want to put myself in ever again!* ’

- ☐ Consider using props. If you practise acupuncture, show the audience the needles so that they can sée how small they are (making sure they are safe – you can put the sharp end into an orange!).

- ☐ In some circumstances you may have to tell people about fire alarms, toilets, breaks, etc. Find out beforehand if you will need to do this.

Making your presentation

- ☐ Begin by thanking your audience for coming.

- ☐ Introduce yourself. Show you are qualified to be giving this presentation but don't bore people with your life history.

- ☐ Tell your audience the format of the presentation (for example, how long it will be, whether you will only be presenting, or whether you will also be demonstrating.)

- ☐ Explain to the audience the rules about asking questions. Should they ask questions when they think of them or keep them until the end of the presentation? If this is one of your first talks I would recommend leaving questions to the end. If you are more confident, you can take questions as they come because this helps to make sure the presentation covers the subjects the audience are most interested in.

- ☐ When you give your presentation, sell a solution to a problem – don't sell your therapy and don't sell yourself. A presentation discussing how you came to your therapy, unless you are already 'famous', is not going to win anyone over. You need to sell a solution, for example, reflexology may help insomnia.

☐ Back up any claims you make about the effectiveness of your therapy with evidence. For example, a recent German study showed that reflexology was effective for some people suffering from insomnia. There is no need to go into too much detail about the study but it is a good idea to have a summary to hand in case anyone is interested at the end of the presentation.

☐ Make sure there is some interaction with your audience. If possible give them something to take away. As a reflexologist I show the audience how to find the reflex points on the hand for the uterus, which is useful for period pain.

☐ Make sure the audience are aware that you know more than you have time to tell them today. If they know the whole story, why should they book a treatment with you?

☐ If they really need a personalized solution, let them know this. You can do this by using a 'case study' of two people with the same complaint, and describe how you treated them both differently because of their individual circumstances.

☐ Bring your presentation to a close with a brief review to provide a satisfactory conclusion.

☐ Make sure that your audience know how to contact you if they have any further questions that may be too personal to ask in front of other people, or would like to book a treatment or buy product. If you have any special offers for the event introduce them now.

☐ Invite questions from the audience.

☐ End your presentation. Thank the audience for their time.

Consider having a prize draw for a full treatment where your audience members provide name, telephone number and email address. The draw should take place some time after your presentation, otherwise people don't have any incentive to leave their number/email. You can then contact the unlucky losers after the event to offer them a special offer as a consolation prize.

Finding your audience

Many groups are happy to have a guest speaker come and talk to them. Decide who would be your ideal client and then consider the following organizations.

- ☐ School parent–teacher associations. Many PTAs run Ladies' Evenings to raise funds for the school. During the evening the ladies are normally offered a glass of wine, there are usually one or two speakers and there may be other vendors selling goods. If you are interested in this kind of venue, approach the chairperson of each of your local PTAs. I have included an example letter which you can use as a basis for your approach in Additional Information Sheet 2, at the end of the book. In any letter make sure that you explain how you see the session working so that if the PTA has not previously run these evenings, they can see how they work and, more importantly, how the PTA can make money from the evening.

- ☐ The Ladies' Circle. Most Ladies' Circle groups meet once a month and invite a speaker to each meeting. It is often a struggle for them to find interesting speakers, so they may welcome an approch from you.

- ☐ The Women's Institute. Details of your nearest WI can often be found in your local paper but, as I mentioned earlier, the age range of the women who attend these meetings can vary enormously so it is definitely worth checking out the members of the group you will be talking to.

- ☐ Local women's groups. There are all sorts of women's groups that have been set up to serve a particular area. You can normally hunt these down from local noticeboards, especially in the library.

- ☐ Mum and Toddler Groups are abundant in most areas so, again, if your target clients are mums, toddlers or slightly older children, these would be good places for you to talk.

- Gyms and health clubs will be full of people interested in their health, who are likely to sustain sporting injuries. If this fits in with your therapy, contact all your local gyms.

- Local old people's organizations. Many ailments are age related or worsen as people age. There are plenty of organizations set up to help this section of the population, such as the Older People's Forum.

- The National Childbirth Trust organize pre- and post-natal meetings for expectant and new mums, so if your clients are likely to be pregnant, have just given birth, or you are interested in treating babies and toddlers, try approaching the NCT.

- Most areas have carers' groups, where unpaid carers, who can be men, women or children, meet to chat and support each other. They are always receptive to any suggestions on how to reduce stress, and some of them could become your clients.

- The Church. You may consider approaching your local church or Christian group.

- Some ethnic groups hold meetings and are pleased to have speakers.

- Many organizations have Annual General Meetings where they invite a speaker in order to try and encourage more people to attend the meeting. If you have identified any suitable organizations, ask if you could be invited to speak. I have spoken at our local preschool playgroup during their AGM.

- Many businesses like to show that they are concerned with their employees' health. There may be some in your area where the employees seem a good match for you as potential clients. If so, ask if there could be an opportunity for you to speak to a group of employees. Sometimes it is possible to arrange a talk during a lunch hour. These are generally better attended than sessions after work.

- Singles organizations. Not all singles clubs are about dating. Many are more interested in arranging interesting outings and events and could be well worth approaching.

Targeting your presentation

Although I have made this point before, it is worth reapeating. You can increase the number of people who might be interested in your talk by targeting your presentation towards specific health or lifestyle problems. For example, some people may be interested in having a talk on reflexology, but many more might be interested in learning how they can reduce stress or manage health problems specific to women.

> *Judy managed a clinic based in a health club. To try and find new clients for the clinic, she arranged a talk called 'The Complementary Guide to Women's Health'. Tickets were sold for the event but all of the ticket revenue went towards the glass of wine or soft drink that each attendee was entitled to. Judy arranged for three of the clinic therapists, a homeopath, a physiotherapist specializing in women's health and a reflexologist, to talk. The event was very well attended, with the women seeking advice about a variety of problems, especially those associated with menstruation, the menopause and fertility. As far as the event was concerned, the clinic broke even, but each of the speakers gained several new clients, which was the real aim of the evening.*

OFFERING FREE TREATMENTS

In my opinion, free treatments should not be given, other than in very exceptional circumstances. If you give somebody a free treatment then they don't value it. To make this work you must ensure that the person receiving the treatment doesn't perceive it as free. One way to do this is to offer a treatment voucher as a raffle prize at a local event or, if you are starting work at a business site, offer the manager vouchers for treatments to be given as rewards to staff.

When I first started as a therapist lots of my family and friends received treatment vouchers for birthday and Christmas presents. In this way I was saving myself money by not having to buy presents, keeping myself busy as a therapist (because in the beginning it can be disheartening if you haven't treated anybody all week) and carrying out marketing, because my voucher clients were thrilled with their treatments and told all their friends (although I must admit I encouraged them to do this!).

Promoting yourself through the media

The media includes television, radio, newspapers and magazines. The problem for a new therapist starting work or opening a clinic is to come up with an angle that is newsworthy. The best way to get your therapy or clinic featured in the media is to relate your business to something that is currently in the news. For example, if a famous sports personality has suffered an injury and you know that your therapy has been effectively used on other occasions to treat the same injury, send out a press release explaining how your therapy 'could' help the personality. If there is any research that could corroborate your claim, include it as an addendum to your press release.

PAYING FOR ADVERTISING

Paid for advertising, whether on the radio, TV or in newspapers or magazines, is intended to persuade people to buy your product. There is no magic wand though when it comes to advertising. Many well-known brands spend an immense amount of money on advertising. However, although many of the adverts we see in our papers and magazines may be memorable as advertisements, we don't necessarily always remember exactly which product is being advertised. Try the exercise below.

Exercise

Choose a couple of well-known magazines and cut out 20 advertisements, taking care to remove anything which will identify the brand name of the product being advertised. So, for example, if you cut out a picture of a famous model advertising face cream, keep the picture of the model but remove the brand name. When you have cut out all 20, ask ten friends to name the brands. With the amount of money spent on advertising by the top brands, you would expect most of your friends to be able to correctly name most of the brands.

The results of my advertising game were . . .

....

....

If major brands, with their huge budgets, struggle to make you remember their names, think about how much harder the job is for you, with what is normally a very limited budget and almost always a lack of time.

Generally, advertisements in local newspapers are not effective for common relaxation therapies, and adverts for massage therapists, however carefully worded, can attract the wrong sort of client. However, advertising a service that has not previously been available locally can be more successful. So, for example, a podiatrist advertising a new business in an area where there is no local competition may have good results. If you can persuade your local paper to write a short feature about your business, this too can be more effective than paying for an advertisement.

> *Julia was starting out in her therapy business and was approached by a journalist from a locally distributed magazine. The journalist came to Julia, had a treatment and then wrote about the treatment in the magazine. Julia wasn't charged for the feature, but she was asked to take out a paid advertisement on another page in the magazine. This worked really well for Julia and she picked up a number of clients. But it was the feature that paid dividends, not the advert. It is definitely something she would do again.*

If you are considering paying for an advertisement in a local newspaper or magazine, ask the following questions:

1. What are the costs of placing different-sized advertisements?

2. Are there any discounts available for first-time advertisers?

3. Is colour an option?

4. Are discounts available if you advertise over several weeks?

5. Is there a particularly good day/week/month to place your advert?

6. Are they running any features which you could place your advertisment next to? For example, some papers regularly run features on women's health or complementary medicine.

The timing of your advertisement may be important. For instance, just before Christmas may not be a good time to advertise unless you can sell vouchers which can be used as Christmas presents. Can you capitalize on Mother's Day, Valentine's Day, people wanting to slim for their summer holidays, or get fit for their winter skiing holiday?

Radio adverts can be effective but they are generally very expensive and cover a much wider geographical area than is relevant for individual therapists. As with newspapers and magazines, it makes sense to stay local. If the radio station you have chosen covers Hampshire, but clients generally wouldn't travel more than ten miles to visit you, most of the people hearing the advertisement are never going to become clients. This type of advertising is generally not very cost-effective for most therapists.

WRITING ARTICLES AND MAKING GUEST APPEARANCES

If you can write a magazine article, or be a guest on a radio show talking about your therapy, you can easily be seen as the 'expert' and greatly increase your profile. These are not easy options. You need a good standard of English and to be able to write about your therapy from an interesting and hopefully unusual angle. If you are a guest on the radio you will need lots of confidence and excellent presentation skills, but if that is you, and you are passionate about your therapy, go for it.

' *When I had recently qualified I was interviewed on Classic FM about my reflexology practice. Although I didn't secure any clients directly as a result of this interview, I was surprised how many people had heard me on the radio and I definitely think that it helped to raise my profile in the local area.* '

Promoting yourself through existing clients

Your existing clients are your best promotional resource, so the first thing to do is ask your clients if they know anyone who would benefit from your therapy. If your clients are happy with their treatments, most will be willing to recommend you. You can also consider the following ideas.

OFFER DISCOUNT VOUCHERS

If a client knows somebody who might be interested in a treatment with you, offer them a discount voucher to pass on. To ensure your existing client doesn't feel they are missing out, make it clear on the voucher that the discount is only valid for new clients and only for the first treatment.

OFFER CLIENTS DISCOUNTED GIFT VOUCHERS

This works well if you are offering a relaxation or pampering type of treatment. So for, example, if you normally charge £20 for Indian Head Massage, you can offer to sell your clients gift vouchers for a reduced amount, for example, £15. This way your client spends less on the gift, but the recipient receives a full-price treatment. You can specify that the recipient must not be an existing client of yours.

OFFER CLIENTS INCENTIVES

You have to be very careful when offering incentives to clients for recommending you, as the potential client may feel that the recommending client is only making the recommendation so that they can gain from the transaction.

> *A therapist in my area offered his existing clients a free treatment if they sent him four new clients. I was interested in trying out this particular therapy and I did take the therapist's details from the person recommending him. However, when the recommending client told me that if I booked in, as I was his fourth referral, he would get a free treatment, it put me off and I didn't book. However, I have sent flowers or a box of chocolates to existing clients of mine who have recommended me to their friends because I think a thank you is always nice.*

CIRCULATE NEWSLETTERS

Newsletters can be used to rekindle interest in clients who have stopped coming to see you, by informing them of any new treatments you are offering. Some therapists include an offer in their newsletter, but it is more important to include something that may be of interest to your clients, or they may see the offer simply as a way of selling to them. As an example, during winter an aromatherapist might recommend an essential oil to help with the snuffles. In March, a homeopath could remind clients to start their hay fever remedy. In the early summer, a nutritionist may recommend a diet or eating regime to help clients shape up for summer. And a pilates instructor might be talking to her clients in December about getting their leg muscles ready for skiing. If your clients feel they are receiving useful and relevant information, rather than simply promotional material, they are much more likely to read your newsletter.

Using third parties

There are a number of third parties who can help you build up your practice. Many health food shops will be happy to stock leaflets from complementary therapy practitioners. Some GPs will agree to either refer clients, especially if your therapy is supported by research, or display a poster or

leaflets in their surgery. You could have an agreement with another practitioner to refer clients to each other. For example, beauty therapists offering pedicures could refer clients to a podiatrist. A physiotherapist could refer clients to a massage therapist to complete their clients' recovery.

You don't have to limit yourself to other therapists. For example, I know of a wedding dress supplier who stocks leaflets and recommends a beautician specializing in bridal make-up, in exchange for a discount on her regular tanning sessions.

Using the Internet and email

When I first qualified, I was the only student in my group to have a website. And, to be fair, in 2001 a website wasn't a necessity. However, things have now changed and with so many people using the Internet to find therapists, everyone should have a website and allow prospective clients to contact them via email. After personal recommendation, or actually meeting potential clients, a website is the next best way of promoting yourself. It is your selling tool.

> ' *Cathy is an established practitioner offering a number of different therapies. She has always advertised with the Yellow Pages, and regularly taken out adverts in the local paper. Recently she has experienced a drop in the number of clients she has been seeing. In the past, this would have been the prompt for her to place more advertisements in different papers, but since attending my 'Creating Clients' course, whenever she has had a new client she has asked them how they found her details. Cathy discovered, that apart from those who had a personal recommendation, all of her new clients had found her on the Internet. So, although initially her advertising may have benefited her, in the past 12 months she hadn't picked up a single client but had spent well over £500.* '

INTERNET REGISTER OF THERAPISTS

Most therapy organizations now have an online directory which will allow prospective clients to find therapists. You should ensure you are registered with this directory and include a link to your own website. Generally, a prospective client will give their location and the website will display several nearby therapists. If your own website is linked into this site, the prospective client can look at it and decide if they want to call you. There are no figures available for this, but from anecdotal evidence I believe that if you have a website, you are much more likely to be called by a prospective client than if they only see your name and location.

There are lots of independent therapist directories, such as www.worldwide-health.com. If the directory is free, you should definitely register. The only downside is that you might receive some unsolicited mail.

If you have to pay to register on a site, ask yourself the following questions:

1. What is the focus of the site? If it is biased towards beauty and you are offering a complementary therapy, then you are not going to get many, if any, referrals from the site.

2. How many therapists in your area are on the site? If the number is small this means either the site is new or is not being marketed effectively. If the site is new, you shouldn't be subsidizing it while it builds up its business. If it is not being marketed effectively, then it won't bring you new clients.

3. How many therapists are offering the same therapies as you? It may seem to be an advantage to be the only person on the register offering hot stones, but in practice clients want a choice and will go elsewhere.

4. How up to date is the therapist information? The best way to find this out is to pick a number of therapists at random and contact them, some by email, some by phone. I would contact at least ten therapists by email as this is the information that is most often out of date, and at least five therapists by phone. Tell them where you found their details, and say you are thinking about using the site. Ask them if they are happy with the site, and most importantly, how many clients they think they have gained from the site. However, it is surprising how many therapists don't ask potential clients where they found their details.

5. How easy is it to find the site? If you search on the Internet and you can't find the site without typing in their address, then your potential clients won't be able to find it either.

INTERNET REGISTER OF BUSINESSES

There are a lot of these, such as yell.com. Generally, you won't gain a lot of business from these sites but as long as your entry is displayed on the first page of the listing you will get some business. As an additional benefit, because you are able to input your website address into these sites, it will help your ranking with Google and other search engines.

SOCIAL NETWORKING SITES

Sites such as Facebook and Twitter can be used as part of your publicity if your clients use these sites. Generally, social networking sites are used by younger people.

When you are first qualified you can talk about how excited you are to have passed your exams, you can replace your picture with one of you wearing your therapist's uniform, and you can update your friends on your new clients, taking care to include nothing that breaches client confidentially. This can work very well when you are first qualified, but as you become established it would be very tiresome for your Facebook friends, so use this facility sparingly and with care.

Following hot topics on Twitter, or forums such as those at www.worldwide-health.com, allows you to both understand what your prospective clients think about the issues being discussed and offer advice. As with Facebook above, use this sparingly. You don't want to spend all of your time answering questions and giving free advice. However, you can give advice or your opinion where you think it will help to build up your reputation or generate business. Just don't overtly sell because this is the quickest way to put off potential clients.

Facebook has an events section which you can use and I tested it out recently when I organized a charity health and wellbeing fair. It was very successful because I asked all of the therapists exhibiting at the event to put themselves on Facebook as attending the fair. Because it was a charity event, many people were quite happy to talk about the event or say they would be attending. This generated the numbers I needed to really get things moving. If you are using this facility to advertise an open day at your new clinic you need to work on your numbers. So, as well as inviting all of your Facebook friends, I would ring them up and ask them to help out by talking about the event and agreeing to attend or writing a nice note to explain why they are unable to come.

EMAIL

Email is a great way of keeping in touch with clients, and an email newsletter is good because, apart from your time to create and send it, there are no costs involved. However, if you use email you must ensure you check it regularly, at least twice a day. As a therapist I know that if I get an email enquiry I have a couple of hours to respond at the most,

after which time another therapist will have responded and probably picked up the business. If you think about the way you look for suppliers, you don't just email one person and wait to see if they reply. You email half a dozen and the first one to reply will generally get your business.

You can't just email anybody – it is illegal. So you must build up your own list of emails addresses. You can start with all your existing clients or case study clients. Make sure you ask for clients' email addresses on your consultation form. Then, each time you attend an event, for example a health fair, or give a talk, you can organize a raffle. The prize can either be a treatment, if your therapy is suitable, or something else to do with your therapy. To enter the raffle people must give their name, telephone number and email address. You will need to include a line explaining that you won't pass on their email address to anyone else (this is necessary and reassuring for them) and giving them the option of not being added to your distribution list. Also, each email you send out should include a line giving the recipient the option of being removed from your distribution list. Although distribution lists take a little while to build up, they are definitely worth doing.

Confidentiality is very important. If you send out a news letter or other communication via email, make sure you keep your list of email addresses confidential. When you send your email, send it to yourself and 'blind copy' everyone else on your list. By blind copying, none of your recipients can see anyone else's email address. This is very important because it is annoying to have your details sent to lots of people you don't know, and the whole aim of this exercise is to get your client's attention, not to annoy them so that they ask to be removed from your list.

Exercise

Start building up your email distribution list.

If you use Microsoft Outlook, when you create a new message and the blind copy tab, which is 'Bcc', is not displayed, select 'Options' and then select the Bcc tab. Bcc should now be displayed on your new message. Any email addresses in the Bcc tab will receive the email, but their address will not be visible to anyone else receiving it.

INTERNET ADVERTISING

You can advertise on the Internet in many ways, including Google pay-per-click and Facebook. You need to make your advertisement snappy, so if you are a chiropractor, don't head your advert with 'New Chiropractor', choose something that will make potential clients click on it such as 'Suffering from back pain?' Some of the sites, such as Facebook, allow you to choose the gender and age of the people who will see your advertisement. So, looking back to the section on who your clients are, make sure you are reaching the right people. For example, I recently advertised one of my training courses on Facebook to females who spoke English and were 25 and older. What you must do with any Internet advertising is to make sure that your advertisement is only displayed in the areas your clients come from. So, in the example above, the advertisement was only displayed to English-speaking females who were 25 and older and who lived within 60 miles of Southampton.

How to make people want your therapy

Remembering what first attracted you to your therapy or product can give you a head start in trying to attract clients to your business.

Exercise

Remember your first treatment/use of product – what made you try it?

....

What made you go back for a second treatment/visit?

....

What was it about the therapy/product that made you want to train as a practitioner/ sell the product?

....

What do you love about your therapy/product?

....

....

....

SELLING THE BENEFITS OF YOUR THERAPY

In all your literature, presentations, and every time you talk about your therapy or product, you need to make your potential clients want to experience your therapy, and anticipate the beneficial effects of your treatment. Will they feel completely relaxed? Will they be pain free? Will they be delighted when they look in a mirror and see a revitalized, flawless complexion? Will they feel full of energy? Will they be refreshed? Will all of their stress have ebbed away?

Exercise

Take a moment to jot down the five most prominent feelings your clients will have after they have received a treatment from you.

1.

....

2.

....

3.

....

4.

....

5.

....

There is an old saying that salespeople work to 'sell the sizzle, not the sausage'. In the same way, you are not selling your therapy, you are selling a benefit. So look at your therapy and consider what are its benefits.

Exercise

List the benefits your client will experience if they take advantage of your therapy/ product. Think of this always from the client's point of view.

1.

....

2.

....

3.

....

4.

....

5.

....

WHAT MIGHT STOP CLIENTS USING YOUR THERAPY?

There could be a number of reasons why people might not want to book a treatment with you. It could be the cost, or that your therapy is not endorsed by the medical profession, or that they are unable time off work. It could even be that they are worried about undressing in front of a stranger, or are afraid of pain during the treatment. Whatever the barriers are, you need to identify them and, where possible, remove them.

I was trying to persuade a potential client to come and have a reflexology treatment with me. I knew the person loved having her feet massaged, so I couldn't work out why she was so reluctant to book in for a treatment. Eventually, I asked her outright what was stopping her. Her answer really surprised me. She was worried that I would pick up something on her feet that would show she had a medical problem. I explained that you cannot use reflexology to diagnose, but I also agreed with her that during her treatment, when I found an area which was bumpy or out of balance, I wouldn't talk to her about the area on the body this was related to. The person became a client and really enjoyed her treatments.

Exercise

Take a couple of minutes and list the barriers that might stop people trying your therapy. The consider how you might be able to remove each barrier.

Barrier	How to remove the barrier
1.	
2.	
3.	
4.	
5.	

WHAT ARE THE OBJECTIVES OF YOUR PROMOTIONAL MATERIAL?

Before you begin writing your leaflets, the text for your website, or any other marketing material, you must have a clear objective. Ask yourself, what do you want your document/advertisement/literature to achieve?

Exercise

Write down the objectives of your promotional material and refer to them whenever you write anything which potential clients will see.

My objectives for all my promotional material are:

1.

2.

....

3.

....

4.

....

5.

....
_____

☐ Tell the reader about the benefits of your therapy but don't dwell on the technicalities. Most prospective clients won't understand them.

☐ Try to address any identified barriers to your treatment. For example, if a reflexologist has discovered that some people believe having reflexology involves removing clothes, in her leaflet, she can specifically state that the client would only need to remove shoes and socks.

☐ Aim for a relaxed, informal style. Write as if you are talking to your potential client.

☐ Back up your claims. This is crucial because, firstly, you mustn't contravene the Trade Descriptions Act and secondly, it is important that you sound trustworthy and believable.

☐ Don't give the reader too many options – this confuses them.

☐ Don't crowd your space – leave lots of white space to allow your message to make an impact.

☐ Check your spelling and formatting. Poor spelling and sloppy grammar looks unprofessional and creates a bad impression of your business.

☐ Make your prose active and persuasive so that your reader feels they cannot miss out on your treatment. Instil a sense of urgency, then tell them what to do: 'Book a treatment today by calling this number.'

☐ Most importantly, be passionate about your therapy and let your enthusiasm shine through in everything you write.

Using endorsements and testimonials

Endorsements and testimonials are a great way to sell your product/services. It is reassuring for a prospective client to see that somebody else is happy enough with the service/product to put their name to a recommendation. There are a couple of rules that it is best to follow to increase their effectiveness.

☐ Use full names and enough of the person's address to seem realistic. For example, a recommendation from Mrs Jackie James from West End, Southampton, would be more believable than a recommendation from Mrs J from Hampshire. Who do you think is more likely to exist? Some people are happy for you to use their website or email address (this mostly happens when they themselves are offering services or products) and, if this is the case, you both benefit.

☐ Celebrity endorsements are always good and they don't have to be from national celebrities. What about local sportsmen and women? A professional footballer from your home team may not necessarily be well known nationally, but would make a very believable reference for your sports massage.

☐ Recently dated endorsements are most credible because this shows you are still doing good work.

How the experts sell

Exercise

Watch the Shopping Channel for 20 minutes.

If an advertisement shown on the Shopping Channel is ineffective it won't last long, so most of the advertisements you see will be working very well. They will be doing their job of persuading people to part with their money. And that, after all, is what you are also trying to do.

Notice how:

☐ They use emotion.

☐ They set up a problem – often one you didn't know you had – and then give you the solution.

☐ They use endorsements/testimonials.

- ☐ They reveal the price.

- ☐ They give you a money-back guarantee so you are risking nothing.

- ☐ They use special offers.

- ☐ They play on limited stock availability.

There is no one way of making people want to try your therapy, but if you believe in it and are passionate about it, that will show in everything you do.

6
YOUR PLAN FOR PROMOTION

To give your new business the best possible chance of success, you need to build a plan for promotion so that nothing is forgotten. It doesn't have to be difficult or complicated, but your business is more likely to take shape if you have a definite plan to work to.

Drawing up your plan

When you are compiling your list of actions, include everything that you need to do, no matter how large or small. Use the list below as a base but add anything else you can you think of or leave out anything that is not relevant to you.

PROMOTIONAL MATERIAL

1. Leaflets   Design a leaflet for each of your therapies and a summary leaflet that details all of your therapies.

2. Posters   Design a basic poster that can then be easily modified to promote the opening of your clinic, your therapies or, for example, gift vouchers for Mother's Day.

3. Aftercare leaflet   Your aftercare leaflet is part of your promotion so it should be produced with the same care as you produce the rest of your promotional material.

4. Price list   This should list your permanent prices, not any discounted prices. The latter should always be achieved with a voucher.

5. Business cards   These are available most cheaply on the Internet but also from many print shops. Some therapists have appointment slots printed on the reverse of their business cards.

6. Gift vouchers   You can either design and print these yourself or you can buy quality vouchers from the Internet or printers.

7. Client letters   Design a letter to your case study clients informing them you are qualified and thanking them for their help.

8. Discount vouchers   Offer these to your case study clients and to friends and relatives to help start your business. Make sure you include a 'valid until' date on them because you don't want to be offering discounts once you are busy.

9. Newsletter   Design a newsletter that can be used to promote your business. Every time you send it out you will be able to update it with items which will add value to your readers, as well as information about any promotions you are offering.

INTERNET

1. Website   Choose a website supplier, agree the design and ensure that search engines can find your site.

2. Register   Register your website with all free listings sites.

3. Email   Start building an email distribution list of clients and other people interested in your therapy.

4. Networking   Update your social networking sites with your new career.

5. Advertise   On the Internet, for example, on Google or Facebook.

ACTIONS

1. Carry out a leaflet drop. Decide how many leaflets but go for at least 1,000. Plan a second leaflet drop three weeks after the first.

2. Send a letter to your case study clients enclosing a discount voucher and price list.

3. Put up posters publicizing the opening of your new clinic/treatment room.

4. Send a note to all your friends offering them a discount for their first treatment and the chance to buy discounted gift vouchers.

5. Hold an open day at your clinic or treatment room.

6. Ensure you have your free entry in *Yellow Pages* or *Thomson Local Directory*.

7. Arrange to talk about or demonstrate your therapy. This is a great way of finding clients, so try to do as many as possible of these.

8. Network with other therapists in your area and identify any therapists you could work with, each referring clients to the other.

9. Identify any third parties in your area who could help promote your business.

10. Persuade a friend to hold a pamper evening where their friends try out your therapies.

11. Exhibit at health and well-being events.

12. Advertise in local publications.

13. Ask clients you have treated to give you a reference or approach a local celebrity and offer them a treatment in return for a comment you can use.

14. Submit articles about your therapy/product for local publications.

15. Approach local media and offer to talk about your therapy or product.

Compiling your initial plan

Your plan can be as simple or as detailed as you like. Look at the following options:

☐ You can use a simple list.

☐ You can use a simple list but make sure the urgent items, or those that will take some time to complete, such as producing a website, are at the top of the list.

☐ You can mark each item with a priority. When you are running your own business you never have enough time. By ranking each item as a high, medium or low priority, you can ensure that anything you don't get around to comes from the low priority list.

☐ For each item you can include

  ☐ an estimate of how long it will take you;

  ☐ a start date;

  ☐ a finish date.

Exercise

Produce your own plan for promotion. Use the following example form as a starting point.

Item	Priority	Time required	Start date	End date
1				
2				
3				
4				
5				
6				
7				
8				
9				
10				

Preparing your quarterly marketing plan

Even once you have produced your initial plan, you cannot simply sit back and forget it. Marketing is something you need to do constantly so that you are always attracting new clients to your business. Each quarter, consider the following.

1. How many people are looking at your website? Your website supplier should be able to give you this information. If the figure is too low, you know the search engines are not picking it up so you need to do some work there.

2. Have you carried out a recent search on the Internet for your therapy, to see if you need to add your details to any new register of practitioners?

3. Have you arranged an event, such as exhibiting at a health event or giving a talk on your therapy? You should do this at least each quarter.

4. Are you monitoring how your new clients heard about you? If any advertising comes up for renewal during the quarter, only renew if it has been effective.

Exercise

Produce your own quarterly marketing plan and mark in your diary the dates you will carry it out.

Preparing your yearly marketing plan

Each year you need to reassess your business. You should consider the following points:

1. Review your competition. Have any new therapists started business in your area? Have any existing therapists stopped trading?

2. Check your prices against your competitors' to ensure you are not overpriced or selling too cheaply.

3. Carry out a survey of your clients. Are you still providing the service they want?

4. Check all of your online entries, for example, yell.com. Ensure the information is still valid.

5. Check the effectiveness of all your promotional activities and consider discontinuing the least effective unless they are free and/ or no effort. This is a really important step, but most therapists don't carry it out and end up paying hundreds of pounds a year for advertising that doesn't work and website optimization that they don't need. Find out what marketing works for you and increase it. Then cut out anything that doesn't work.

6. Constantly promote your business, not just during the first few months of its life.

Exercise

Produce your yearly marketing plan.

‘ *Pauline worked hard to promote her massage business and was very successful, finding many new clients. However, after three months her client numbers started to fall. Although initially Pauline had worked hard at marketing, once she started getting clients she sat back. As clients stopped visiting her, often because her treatment has resolved their problem. Pauline did nothing to generate new clients, so her numbers fell.* ’

How do your clients hear about you?

The only way to discover the answer to this question is to ask your clients. When people first contact you, even if they don't book a treatment, ask them how they heard about you. This will help you see which of your promotions are working. You should also note down those clients that actually book with you.

Exercise

Set up a system, similar to the one shown below, to record how your new clients hear about you.

	Number of enquiries	Number of clients
Personal recommendation		
Yellow Pages or other directory		
Leaflet drop		
Stand at exhibition		
Website		

Keep your appointments diary near to the phone. Whenever you receive a telehone enquiry about a treatment, ask the caller how they heard about you and write this down in the back of your diary. If the caller then goes on to book a treatment, note this down too. After all, it doesn't matter how many enquiries you receive, it's actual bookings you need.

Although, generally, marketing which involves you meeting prospective clients is the most effective, different types of marketing will be more effective for different types of therapist. It is important to remember that more expensive forms of marketing won't necessarily generate you more clients. And look at the cost in terms of not only money, but also your time.

It is important that you continue to check which is the best marketing method for you. You should do this annually, at the very least. By checking what works and what doesn't, you can change what you do to get results. For example, if you aren't picking up any clients through personal recommendation, why is this? Are you asking people to recommend you? If your website isn't bringing you new clients, is it because clients can't find it? Check this yourself. Using Google or your preferred search engine, enter the name of your therapy and your location. If your website does not appear then your clients won't be able to find you either.

In the end, though, if a particular form of advertising isn't working for you, unless it is really costing you nothing, then stop using it. You are wasting your time and money.

7
SETTING UP YOUR BUSINESS

In this chapter we will look at choosing your business name and avoiding some of the common pitfalls that complementary therapists fall into. We will then look at choosing your business model. Many therapists, once they are qualified, automatically think that their only options are to be self-employed or to work for an employer such as the NHS or a spa. So, before choosing your business model, you need to understand the implications of each.

Finding a name for your business

From the first time a potential client hears the name of your business they will instantaneously make assumptions about you. Choosing a name is a very important first step, but it is one of the things you may find most difficult.

Here are some of the things you should think carefully about:

☐ What therapies or services do you plan to offer? I have known many therapists who have decided on a name based on the first therapy they have learnt. For example, a newly qualified reflexologist might call her business 'Fabulous Feet'. This is definitely a positive-sounding name. But let's look at this person 12 months later. They are successful with their reflexology but they have added Indian head massage to their list of therapies. The name 'Fabulous Feet' is now not so appropriate, but they may have invested a considerable amount of money in that name. They will probably have business stationery and a website, they may even have had a logo produced. All of the money spent on these items would now be wasted if the therapist changed the name of their business. In addition, they would also lose the reputation of the name. Knowing what therapies and services you are likely to offer in the future, before you choose your name, can save you a lot of money and effort.

☐ What is important to you about your therapies? When a prospective client hears the name of your business they immediately start to build up a picture of what the business is like. So you should use this to reinforce those aspects of your therapy that are important to you. In business you should never miss an opportunity to differentiate yourself and show how you are better than your competitors, and that can start with your name.

Think also about your aim in giving a treatment. For many therapists there is only one aim, you are trying to improve your clients' health. For others though you do get to make a choice. If you call yourself 'Sara's Health and Beauty Therapies', the fact that you include beauty gives people the impression, rightly or wrongly, that you as a therapist have less focus on health. Similarly, if you call yourself 'Relaxing Therapies', a client with a bad back is less likely to choose you than a therapist calling themselves the 'Alton Back Clinic'.

☐ What do you hope to be doing in the long term? It may seem too early to think about what you will be doing in ten years' time, but if you know where you will be in the future, you can start with a name that will cover both what you are doing now and what you hope to be doing in the future. You can change the name at a later date, and many businesses do, but if you can choose a name at the start and stick to it, every single client who goes through your practice will know that name. This means that ten years down the line, when you open up a clinic with the same name, anyone who has ever had a treatment with you will immediately know the new clinic is you.

☐ Are you going to use your own name in your business? This can be very successful, but if you are going to employ other therapists to treat clients, or you think you may want to sell your business in the future, consider this carefully. If you have high aspirations for your business, naming it after yourself might not be the best thing to do. Let's imagine you offer sports massage. You lease a room and call your business 'Sports Massage by Tania'. You are good at both massage and marketing and soon find that you have more clients than you can handle. You are limited by the number of hours you can work a day, but you have the use of your room for many more hours, so you ask a friend to help you out a couple of days a week. This can work really well, but some clients, finding their masseuse is Sally, rather than Tania, might feel short-changed! Tania then decides to sell her practice, but unless she can find another Tania to sell to she could end up in trouble. If it has been a successful business then Tania must have been an important part of it, her name and presence have been vital to her success. By selling the practice without the name she will be losing some of the goodwill. All she can sell in reality is her client base, worth considerably less than a full business.

☐ Where will your name appear in an alphabetical list of therapists? If your business is Amanda's Aromatherapy Clinic, you may well find yourself at the top of any list. If your business name is Yasmine's Holistic Therapies, you could find yourself at the end of the list. This is less of a problem with printed directories like the Yellow Pages, but with search engines such as Google, prospective clients very rarely get past the first page.

Exercise

Look at the following business names. None is the name of an actual business, but some of them are quite close. Write down what the name tells you about each business and what sort of clients would be attracted to that business. For this exercise it is important to jot down your first impressions, so don't spend too long thinking.

Hollies Holistic and Beauty Therapies

Better Healthcare

Reflexology for Relaxation

Cura Healthcare

Aromatherapy for Better Health

Janet Taylor

Tranquil Time Holistic Therapies

Janet Taylor Homeopath

Janet Taylor Complementary Therapist

Top to Toe

Janet Taylor Holistic Therapist

Nicki's Beauty and Massage Rooms

Pampered Feet

New Age Complementary Therapy

Sole Solutions

Sports Massage by Mary

Restorative Reflexology

Relaxing Therapies

REVIEW OF THE EXERCISE

Names will always mean different things to different people. Some people will like a name, others will hate it. You cannot hope to choose a name that has the right connotations for everyone, but you should think about eliminating obvious problems.

Twenty people were asked about the names in this exercise. They were asked what the name 'said' to them about the business, if they would be likely to book a treatment with that business and, if the name contained a reference to a specific treatment, if they would book a different treatment with that business.

Below is a selection of their responses:

- ☐ **Hollies Holistic and Beauty Therapies** Testers thought this would be a nice friendly place to visit but weren't sure about booking in if they had a specific health problem.

- ☐ **Better Healthcare** Several testers thought that this sounded like something run by the NHS. Most testers thought it was a clinic offering a variety of therapies, or an insurance company.

- ☐ **Cura Healthcare** Generally testers found the claim to 'cure' unrealistic, so most testers would shy away from booking with this business.

- ☐ **Janet Taylor** Respondents generally wondered what this therapist did, although one tester thought that because she was just using her name she must have a good reputation.

- ☐ **Janet Taylor Homeopath** Testers liked this name as it was personal and most would book a homeopathy consultation with Janet. However, if Janet did offer other therapies, they would be much less likely to book, say, an Indian head massage with her.

- ☐ **Janet Taylor Complementary Therapist** Most testers generally wondered what this therapist did. The 'complementary' was generally well received, but a few testers didn't understood what 'complementary' meant and so would be put off by this name.

- ☐ **Janet Taylor Holistic Therapist** Testers were definitely in two camps with this name. Those that understood the term 'holistic' thought it was a great name, but not all testers understood the term correctly and some were definitely put off by it, thinking it was somehow negative.

☐ **Pampered Feet** Testers liked this name and when asked what they thought the therapist offered, most said pedicures. They would be very likely to book a pedicure with Pampered Feet but less so a therapy such as reflexology or podiatry.

☐ **Sole Solutions** This name had mixed reviews, with one tester mistaking Sole for Soul, and another tester thought that maybe the name was a little too clever.

☐ **Restorative Reflexology** Some testers found this name confusing, being unsure what restorative really means, but other testers liked the name.

☐ **Relaxing Therapies** Testers generally liked this name and would be happy to book a relaxing treatment, but if they had a health problem they would try another therapist.

☐ **Aromatherapy for Better Health** Again this name was well received and many testers thought it sounded professional while telling you exactly what the business offered.

☐ **Tranquil Time Holistic Therapies** Testers generally like this name for relaxing therapies although one thought the name was too long.

☐ **Top to Toe** Generally testers weren't sure what this therapist offered, but the consensus of opinion was that it was some form of beauty makeover business.

☐ **Nicki's Beauty and Massage Rooms** Although there is nothing wrong with this business name, 'massage rooms' has bad connotations for some people, so none of the testers would book a treatment with Nicki, and one tester specifically said it sounded 'iffy'.

☐ **New Age Complementary Therapy** Again, this name was not well received, with only one of the testers willing to make a booking with this business. One tester suggested there was a large hint of 'flower power' about this name, and another thought it sounded dated.

☐ **Sports Massage by Mary** Most testers liked this name and would be happy to book a sports massage with Mary, although they would be less likely to book non massage therapies with her. One tester suggested that, as Mary is an old-fashioned name, she might be an older lady, so the massage might be more 'tame'.

Exercise

Think of five different business names you like and feel you could use. Write them down and then ask 20 different people what they think of each name, what sort of business they think it is and if they would consider using them. You will never achieve a 100% positive response, but if your testers don't give you good feedback, rip up your list and start again.

So you've chosen your name

Once you have chosen your name, your next job is to check that nobody else is using it.

Exercise

1. Check your chosen name with Companies House at www.companieshouse.gov.uk. Companies House contains a list of all limited and publically limited companies, so if the business name you want appears on this website you should not use it.

2. Search the Internet. Type your chosen name into a search engine. If you discover that somebody is using that name, but the company is not limited or plc, you may still be able to use it. For example, if you practise in Southampton and the other person practises in Edinburgh, there is unlikely to be a problem for a local therapy business. However, if they are geographically close to you, your two businesses could be confused. For example, you may be scrupulous with hygiene, always give a full treatment and offer value for money. However, if the other business with 'your name', doesn't have such high standards, they may have a poor reputation which could damage your business. You should also be wary of businesses with the same or a similar name which offer different treatments as this can also confuse clients.

3. Use online directories such as yell.com to search for a business with the name you have chosen.

4. Use online directories such as yell.com to search for businesses which offer the same therapies or services as you in your area.

5. Check to see if a website name is available. Unless all your marketing is going to be by word of mouth, an Internet site will be beneficial. It's no good just typing your name into your browser because somebody may have purchased the name but not yet got around to doing anything with it. You need to check www.123reg.co.uk to make sure the name you want is free. If the website name you want is not available, 123reg will give you lots of similar names to consider.

Choosing your business model

In this section we will look at the advantages and disadvantages of being self-employed, working in a partnership, starting a limited company and being an employee. We will also discuss how you can combine these options to get the best out of your therapies.

Working for yourself

Setting up business as a sole trader, or being self-employed, is the simplest way to start your holistic therapy business. All you have to do is inform the Inland Revenue that you are self-employed and you can start trading.

The big advantage of being self-employed is that you don't have to share your profits with anyone, except of course the tax man. You are also free to work when you want and how you want, you can work to your own values and standards, which you need never compromise, and you get to make all of your own decisions.

The downside of working as a self-employed therapist is that you are on your own. This means you are responsible for keeping your own financial records, paying your own tax and insurance, and – as the owner of the business – you are legally inseparable from the business. You are responsible for any losses. This means that if as a business you lose money and run up debts, your own assets can be used to pay those debts.

The only legal formality you need to be aware of as a sole trader is the Business Names Act (1985). This states that if you trade under a different name from your own, you need to make sure that everyone who deals with you is aware that you are the owner of the business.

INCOME TAX

If you are working as a self-employed therapist you must register with the Inland Revenue within the *first three months of full trading*. You need to do this even if you have another full- or part-time job. Some people are nervous about contacting the Inland Revenue but they are very helpful and often have leaflets available to take you through everything you need to do. Once you are registered you will be responsible for paying your own income tax, normally by completing a self-assessment form each year.

> *I run a Creating Clients course for therapists. Normally the course attracts new therapists but on one particular course there were six very established therapists who needed to increase their client numbers. The requirement to register with the Inland Revenue as self-employed is a topic in my course and I started to gloss over it when I realized that half of the group hadn't registered as self-employed. One therapist thought that because she was also employed by a large company she didn't need to register, and the other two believed incorrectly that because their earnings were low enough that they didn't need to pay tax, they didn't need to register either. Both of these assumptions are totally wrong and each therapist could have received a hefty fine.*

NATIONAL INSURANCE

National Insurance contributions entitle employees to benefits such as incapacity benefit, the basic state retirement pension, widow's benefit and maternity allowance. As a self-employed person you are responsible for paying National Insurance monthly or quarterly.

Self-employed people pay two sorts of contributions:

Class 2   These are paid unless you

- ☐ have a small earnings 'Certificate of Exception';

- ☐ are under 16 years of age;

- ☐ are over state pension age;

- ☐ are unable to work in certain circumstances, whether or not you are receiving benefit.

You must also pay Class 2 NICs if you are self-employed in your spare time, even if you are also paying National Insurance as an employee (Class 1). However, if your Class 1 payments exceed a certain level, you may be able to defer payment of your Class 2 NICs.

Class 4   You will also have to pay Class 4 National Insurance if your profits are between £5,715 per year and £43,875 per year (for 2010/11) plus 1% on any profit over that amount.

Exercise

List the advantages and disadvantages of being a self-employed therapist.

	Advantages	Disadvantages
1.	....	....
2.	....	....
3.	....	....
4.	....	....
5.	....	....

REVIEW OF THE EXERCISE

The two lists below are not complete lists of the advantages and disadvantages of being self-employed, but they should get you started.

Advantages

- ☐ Flexibility – you have control over when you work.

- ☐ As a self-employed therapist you have longer to pay your taxes than if you were employed and had to pay as you earn (PAYE).

- ☐ You can work as and where you like.

- ☐ You can apply your own values and standards. (Don't underestimate the importance of this. See the case study of Surinder, later in this chapter).

- ☐ You can brand to suit your own image and style.

- ☐ All the profits are yours.

- ☐ You can gain a lot of personal satisfaction from running your own successful business.

- ☐ This model of business is very easy to set up.

Disadvantages

- ☐ You need to work when your clients are available. If you are working as a physiotherapist, generally clients are quite happy to attend appointments during the day as physiotherapy appointments are seen as a valid reason to miss work. However, if you are offering aromatherapy, working clients are less able to attend during the day so you may find yourself working weekends and evenings.

- ☐ You have to keep good financial records and need to pay your own tax and National Insurance contributions.

- ☐ You have to find all your own clients and are responsible for all of your own marketing.

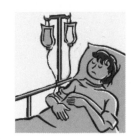

- ☐ There is no sick pay or backup when you are ill.

- ☐ Your earnings can vary from week to week and at different times of the year. Some therapists, especially beauty and pamper therapists, find January a very slow month.

- ☐ You take full personal responsibility for the decisions made for your business and this can be isolating.

- ☐ Sole traders have 'unlimited liability', so they are responsible for all their business debts.

- ☐ You pay your tax at the end of the year, which does seem like an advantage, but you must make sure that you have set money aside for this – and don't spend it!

Working in a partnership

A partnership is when you work with one or more other people and you all share responsibility for running the business. A partnership can be set up without any real legal formalities, but it is sensible to have a 'deed of partnership' drawn up by a solicitor. This should form an agreement which defines the roles and responsibilities of each partner, specifies how the partnership will operate and, importantly, how the profits are split. Without such a document, all partners are said to be 'jointly and severally liable' for the acts and omissions of the other partners when they are acting on behalf of the business. This means that if one partner decides the partnership needs a shiny new location and signs a 10-year lease, all of the partners in the firm are responsible for that lease, even if the partnership cannot afford it. This raises the potential for one partner to lose personal property,

possessions and cash, as a result of the mistakes of another partner. A further problem is that without a deed of partnership profits are split equally between the partners. This is fine if all partners put in an equal amount of work, but if three people work full-time and one person works only two hours a week, the partner working just two hours is on to a very good financial deal.

ADVANTAGES

There are many advantages to working in a partnership. You can pool financial resources and perhaps afford bigger premises than if you were working alone. Partners may support each other and their skills may complement each other. Workload and worries can be shared and there is always somebody there to talk about future plans and ensure all ideas are fully thought out before they are put into action.

DISADVANTAGES

There are some disadvantages to partnerships, even with a deed of partnership in place. Disputes may occur between the partners, who may have very different values. One partner might be quite happy to buy cheap towels and supplies, while another believes that this reflects badly on the practice and would prefer to invest in more expensive materials. One partner could have a vision of the practice being franchised throughout the country, while another is content to work nine to five and has no ambition to grow the business. This can all cause friction between partners.

Another problem can occur if one partner 'values' their own input to the partnership more than that of others. If they are a 'professional therapist', they may feel that their time is more valuable to the partnership than the time of a second partner who manages the clinic and carries out marketing. In the real world, of course, the professional therapist can only work if the marketing partner does their job and brings in clients. All these points need to be discussed and agreed before entering into a professional partnership. Disputes and disagreements can occur even among good friends or family members.

PAYING TAX

You will need to inform the Inland Revenue when you form your partnerships. They are very helpful and have many documents which explain how the tax system works and when you become liable for National Insurance. Your partnership needs to start keeping records of all your expenses and income and you will be required to fill in a tax return every year after which, if you have made enough profit, you will receive a tax bill. You may also be liable for National Insurance payments.

Forming a limited company

There are several different types of limited company but most therapists setting up a business will be looking at private limited companies, where the directors of the business are the shareholders. Shares cannot be sold to the general public; they may only be transferred privately with the prior consent of all existing shareholders. This means you cannot lose control of your business. However, it is more expensive to set up a limited company than to set yourself up as self-employed, and it requires more administration each year. So, if that's the case, why would you need to set up a limited company?

ADVANTAGES

One of the main advantages of setting up a limited company is that your business is separate from you as a person. This mean that if the company is made bankrupt, or is subject to legal action, the losses are limited to the assets of the company, and the directors will not suffer any loss of their personal assets (see the case study below).

It can also look more professional, especially if you are dealing with large companies. For example, if your offers on-site massage to large corporations, that corporation may be more inclined to do business with you than if you were a sole trader.

DISADVANTAGES

On the minus side, there are costs associated with setting up a limited company, you need to submit accounts each year and for most people this means employing an accountant. This financial information can then be inspected by any member of the public, including your competitors.

HOW TO SET UP A LIMITED COMPANY

The easiest way to do this is to ask an accountant you trust to set up the company for you and submit your accounts for a yearly fee. You can, however, set up the company yourself by visiting www.companieshouse.gov.uk and completing form IN01. You will be required to complete a return to Companies House and submit accounts each year. You will also be liable for both corporation tax and personal tax on any profits you make.

‘ *Fiona was a successful self-employed therapist but in order to market her therapies she ran regular health and well-being fairs, where she would sell stands to other therapists. She was running a fair one day in a hall with a stage. Although she had carefully cordoned off part of the stage to ensure that nobody could fall off and injure themselves, Fiona worried that this might happen and that she would be liable, even though she had taken all reasonable precautions for safety. Although she had public liability insurance, she had never fully trusted insurance companies. Then and there Fiona decided to give herself more protection. She investigated the options and found that if she set herself up as a private limited company, she would not be responsible for any losses incurred by that company. Initially she was worried that because she was a sole trader her business wasn't big enough to become a limited company, but this was not a problem.*

Being an employee

As an employee within the NHS, a clinic or a salon, you have lots of advantages. Your wages are guaranteed, whether or not you have clients; you may also be entitled to holiday and sick pay; you will generally be working with other therapists, which can be more interesting for you; and, because you are working regular hours, you will be paid the same amount each week. Also, because your employer takes care of tax and National Insurance, you don't need to put money aside for this each week, which makes it easier for you to budget your household finances. If you are employed as a therapist, generally you will only be responsible for carrying out your therapy. It will be somebody else's job to look after the advertising, answer the phone, keep the accounts and sort out business insurance.

The downside of being an employee is that you have to work to your employer's standards and your employer makes money out of you. Instead of receiving the full amount the client pays for the treatment, you may find yourself earning only slightly more than the minimum wage.

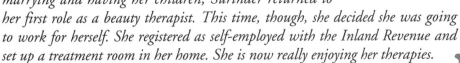

When Surinder left school she worked as a beauty therapist for a small local salon. However, she soon became disenchanted because the owner of the business would 'squeeze' in extra appointments, when there really wasn't the time for Surinder to do a good job. Surinder felt the clients were being short-changed and that this reflected badly on her. Because of her dissatisfaction, Surinder left the beauty industry. However, several years later, after marrying and having her children, Surinder returned to her first role as a beauty therapist. This time, though, she decided she was going to work for herself. She registered as self-employed with the Inland Revenue and set up a treatment room in her home. She is now really enjoying her therapies.

If you want to work as an employee, contact local spas and clinics. Depending on your therapy it might also be worth contacting the NHS.

Working flexibly

Although there are four common options when you are starting out in business – being self-employed, working in a partnership, starting a limited company or being an employee – you need not limit yourself to just one option.

Many practitioners of more mainstream therapies complementary therapists, such as physiotherapy and podiatry, begin by working in the NHS as employees, both for the security it offers and to gain experience. Later they set up their own businesses. Some are fortunate enough to be able to reduce their employed hours on a planned basis, perhaps moving to four days then three days a week, giving their own business time to become established before they are dependent on it to pay the mortgage.

The NHS isn't the only employer of therapists. If you are a massage therapist you may work for a spa or, if you are a beauty therapist or nail technician, you may be employed by a salon. In fact, you don't have to start by working full-time. Many therapists initially try to work two or three days a week as an employee, for security, while they build up their own business in their remaining days.

> *Dave worked as a nurse before training as a sports massage therapist. As his private clients for his therapies increased, so Dave gradually reduced his nursing hours until he felt confident enough to rely on the income from his therapies. He still has his nursing qualification and works occasionally as a contractor, so that he has something to fall back on. However, his business is now so successful that Dave is considering giving up nursing completely, as the few hours he still works as a nurse are preventing him from taking on additional massage clients. Financially it would be much better for Dave to concentrate on his own business.*

8
COSTS AND PRICING

Before you can set your prices you need to understand your costs. If you set your price by plucking a figure out of the air, or matching the prices of other therapists, you run the risk of being unable to make a living from your therapies or, worse still, finding your therapies are costing you money.

In this chapter we will look at both the fixed costs of doing business, and the costs that you incur only when you treat a client.

Fixed costs

These are costs that you will incur no matter how many or how few clients you have. They include the following.

PROFESSIONAL COSTS

☐ Professional and public liability insurance;

☐ Membership of professional organization;

☐ Training. Once you are qualified it is essential to carry on with your training. You need to keep up to date with all new regulations and changes in your chosen therapy. Qualifications such as your first aid certificate will need to be renewed regularly or you may not be able to practise.

LOCATION COSTS

☐ Rent/rates. If you are renting a room or a whole building, you will need to pay your rent and rates, even if you have no clients.

☐ Utilities. If you are buying a building or if you are using a room in your own home you will have to pay utility costs including telephone and Internet.

☐ Redecoration or set-up of your room or building.

MARKETING

☐ Promotion. You may choose to advertise in the local paper, distribute flyers or attend a health fair.

☐ Website. This is a must for any therapist now, and you should include both the initial cost and yearly running costs.

MISCELLANEOUS

- ☐ Any equipment which has to be regularly renewed (i.e. each year) should be included here. As an example, each year I will buy new towels to ensure my stock doesn't look too old. If you play music you may also decide to buy a new CD each year, to give yourself and your customers a change. I also like to buy a new uniform.

- ☐ If you use an accountant, this will be an annual cost.

- ☐ A performing rights licence is required if you play music to your clients. If you are mobile or based in a home treatment room which isn't permanently set up as a treatment room you still need a licence, although a mobile licence will be a little cheaper.

CAPITAL EXPENSES

Some of your expenses, especially your set-up costs, will need to be handled slightly differently from everyday expenses. Capital expenditure is basically for anything that will last the business for more than one year and is an asset of the business. So, if you need to buy a couch, tools, a chair, desk, computer, a desk for your home office, or a printer, these are all items that will last several years, and are treated as an asset of your business. In 2008 there was a change to the way capital expenses are handled. Now, capital expenses up to £50,000 can be claimed each year in a similar way to the way you claim everyday expenses. However, they need to be documented separately, because if you sell any asset once you have claimed tax relief on it, the amount you sell the item for needs to be added to your turnover.

Variable costs

These depend on the number of clients you treat. They can include the cost of couch roll, creams and lotions, surgical spirit or other cleaners, essential oils, nail polish, hand sanitizers, toilet supplies, in fact everything you need to carry out a treatment. Variable costs also include travel if you are mobile or working in a clinic, and even mundane items like washing costs, which are easily overlooked.

It is very easy to underestimate how much it costs to wash your towels and other items. A simple way to check that your costs are about right is to find out how much your washing would cost if you took it to a launderette. This change automatically includes everything, not just the washing powder. The launderette has to include electricity, hot water, maintenance and servicing, wear and tear and eventually the cost of a new washer and dryer or they won't make a profit. So if you use their charge as a guide, you will be about right.

Exercise

Work out your fixed costs and approximate variable costs per client, assuming you treat 500, 1,000 and 1,500 clients in a year.

Fixed costs

....

Variable costs for 500 clients

....

Variable costs for 1,000 clients

....

Variable costs for 1,500 clients

....

Setting a price for your therapy

It is worth spending a little time working out the correct price for your therapy, rather than simply charging the same as everybody else.

You will need the information you collected in Chapters 1 to 3 about you, your clients and your competitors. We will be looking at your location, what is included in your treatment, and at you – how your own personal qualities can add value to your treatment.

Your location

When you are setting your price it is important to compare like with like. If you are treating from an upmarket clinic or health club, clients will generally be happy to pay more than if you are treating from your own living room. If you are a mobile therapist, when working out the cost of a treatment you will need to look at how other therapists include travel costs. This may be totally different depending on whether the therapist is working in an urban environment or a rural environment, where distance between clients will be greater.

Exercise

Look at your treatment rooms from the viewpoint of a potential client. Try to be totally honest with yourself, or ask a friend to give you feedback. Begin your assessment when you drive into your road. From your list of competitors pick out those whose premises are the best match to your own and note down their prices.

What is included in your treatment?

Again, when setting your price it is important that you are comparing like with like. A physiotherapy treatment can last up to half an hour, or up to 20 minutes. The first may initially appear more expensive, but could well work out cheaper in the long run. You should look at what your competitors are including in their treatment price before setting your own. You also need to ensure that your promotion highlights areas where you are offering a service which is better than that of your competitors.

Exercise

Look again at the competitors you highlighted in the previous exercise and compare what is included in their treatments with what you are offering. Where there are differences, try and make adjustments to their prices. For instance, if your competitors are charging £60 for an hour's treatment, and your treatment time is 70 minutes, it is a simple matter of using maths to come up with a £70 equivalent price for what you offer. With other differences it can be more difficult to make adjustments so, rather than trying to cost them, look at their value to the customer and then make your best estimate.

‘ *My dentist has a machine which cuts crowns on the premises. As a person with delicate teeth, I have used this service more than once. My dentist is probably at the top end of the market for my area and his prices reflect that. However, I am happy to pay the additional amount because I know he is always going to have the latest equipment. With the crown machine, I can have my crown designed and fitted in one session. For me, being not too fond of dentists, this is much more preferable than making two visits.* ’

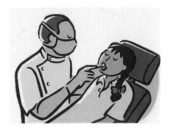

How good are you?

This might seem an odd question because if you are setting up your complementary therapy business you will believe in your therapy and have confidence that you can do a really good job. However, look back to Chapter 1. Is there something in your qualification, or your experience, that would allow you to charge more?

New therapists often start by setting a price which is too low because they are lacking in confidence. However, if you set your prices too low at the start, when you gain confidence and later try to raise them, you could have problems retaining your clients. After all, generally the service they receive from you won't have changed – what will have changed is your level of confidence. So, when you are setting your price, consider what you think you will be worth in 12 months' time. It is your customers' perception of the price that counts – and always remember that price is a sign of quality.

Exercise

Using information from the last three sections, decide how much you are going to charge for your treatment.

Justifying your price

Some say you should never justify your price. I think there are times when you have to, but what you should never do is to apologize for your price or give any indication that you think your treatments are expensive. When 'selling' your therapy/product you should make sure you show your clients where the value is:

- ☐ Up sell – tell prospective clients what is included in your treatment, even if every other practitioner offering your therapy also includes this.

- ☐ Tell prospective clients about any value they cannot see. If you don't tell them, how will they know?

- ☐ Include comparisons with other types of therapy. For instance, if you have a client with a specific problem, for example back pain, and typically you would need to see them for three sessions before they would feel any benefit, you can compare this with a different type of therapy, where the client may require more sessions before they would typically feel some benefit. Even if your prices are more expensive, if you can demonstrate that the client would need to see you for fewer treatment sessions, then you can show that you would be more cost-effective in the long run.

- ☐ Focus on your unique points. Make your client aware of how good you are, but make sure you know too. If you don't believe wholeheartedly in what you are saying to your client, you will give yourself away and they won't believe you either.

Jenny is a very experienced nutritionist who has been practising for over 30 years. After seeing a client she spends three hours analysing their diet and producing a customized report on how they can improve it. Jenny felt that her initial consultation fee looked expensive and was sure she was losing clients because of this. But because each one-hour initial consultation actually took her four hours, she didn't want to reduce her price. However, once she amended her marketing materials and started explaining to prospective clients exactly what was included in their first visit package, she found that nobody queried her price. In fact it worked out at a very low hourly rate and probably should have been higher.

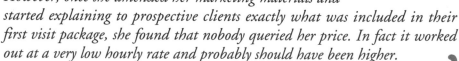

Please ensure that you can back up any claims you make about your therapy or you will be breaking the Trades Description Act as well as bringing your therapy into disrepute. Working as a complementary therapist can be very frustrating because you know your therapy works or you wouldn't be doing it but, unless you have specific proof, please be very careful about what you say.

How to raise your prices

It is important to know how your clients will react to price rises and one way you can do this is to ask them. Although clients won't always give you an honest answer, as they may be too polite, by looking at their body language and really listening to the way they answer (rather than being too keen to hear them say the rise is no problem), you can get a good idea about how they really feel.

By following the rules below, you should be able to raise your prices without impacting your business.

- ☐ Always warn your clients about price rises well before they happen. So, for example, at the beginning of the year you could let your clients know that as of 1 April, prices will rise. If you consistently raise your prices each April, your clients will come to expect it.

- ☐ Avoid raising your prices during a quiet time of the year. For example, as a reflexology practitioner I find that January is always quiet, as people are paying off their credit card bills, and August is quiet as lots of people are on holiday.

- ☐ If a client is in the middle of a course of treatments, consider fixing the price for that course, but letting the client know that if/when they come back to you for the next course, they will have to pay the new fees.

- ☐ Make sure your prices reflect the market. Don't keep the same prices for year after year, then realize your service is too cheap and try to raise your prices by an enormous amount.

Julie is a reflexologist and holistic therapist. Many of her clients come to see her regularly, so when she decided to raise her prices she only raised them for new clients. She didn't anticipate though that some clients would stay with her for a significant amount of time. After she had been practising for six years her reflexology fee was £32. However, she still had several clients who were on the £20 fee she had originally charged when she first qualified. Although these were the people who had helped her build up her business and supported her in her early years, she felt that £20 was no longer a fair exchange for her expertise. Julie did put up her fees but decided that her regular clients would always pay less than new clients. When she put this to her old clients and pointed out the discrepancy between what they were paying and what new clients were paying, and why, they agreed that what she was doing was fair. Julie is now careful not to fall into this trap again.

You can test the market by applying a price rise to new clients only. That way, if you find your supply of new clients dries up, you can quickly put your prices down again without losing credibility with existing clients.

9
FORECASTING AND FINANCE

Calculating your maximum treatment numbers

To calculate the maximum number of treatments you can carry out each week, you could take the number of hours you are working, and divide by your treatment time. So, working a 37-hour week, you could see 37 clients for a one-hour appointment each week. Assuming you work 48 weeks in a year, and you charge £50 per treatment, that would give you a gross revenue (i.e. money in before you have taken your costs out) of $37 \times 48 \times £50 = £88,800$. This is a pretty good salary by any measurement. Unfortunately, things are not quite that easy.

Firstly, many therapies are either physically or mentally demanding, or both, which means that 37 clients in one week would leave you totally exhausted. As a reflexologist, I have never planned to carry out more than 20 reflexology treatments in a week but this figure will be different for different therapies and therapists.

> **TIP** You can use other treatments to increase your working time. For example, I offer Indian head massage, Reiki and Hopi ear candling in addition to the 20 reflexology appointments I have each week. Carrying out an alternative therapy that makes different demands on your body and mind allows you to work more hours overall.

Secondly, unless you work in a clinic with a receptionist who takes the money and rebooks the clients, it is not always physically possible to treat 37 clients in a week. At my home treatment room I allow 15 minutes in between clients to carry out the administration I need to do, rebook and take payment. The 15 minutes is also a buffer in case clients arrive early as I have no waiting room. So, in an eight-hour working day, that 15 minutes would equate to two whole clients. If you are mobile, and have to include travel between clients, the situation is even worse. You might find that in an eight-hour day you can only treat four clients. This can also be a problem for therapists who work in different locations. If you have a clinic in the morning but work in your home treatment room during the afternoon, you will need time to travel between the venues, and that is time when you could be treating a client.

Thirdly, having a therapy business is not all about giving treatments. One of your main activities when you first start practising will be marketing. You will need to spend less time on this as you become more established and more of your clients come to you from personal recommendations, but even experienced therapists have to do some marketing. As a therapist you will also need to complete some additional training to comply with the requirements of your professional body and maintain your registration. Also, all therapists who run their own business have to do their accounts and other administrative tasks such as ordering stock, paying bills and, if you are an employer, dealing with staff.

Forecasting treatment numbers

It is difficut when you first start you your business to forecast how many treatments you will be able to give each month because you have very little to base your figures on. If you look at other similar therapists, you can come up with a figure that's more than just a guess. However, if you ring up somebody offering the same service as you, who practises locally, they may see you as a threat and be reluctant to help you.

You can try the following:

- ☐ Choose an area, not local, which is as similar as possible to the area you will be working in, both economically and socially. Find a therapist in your own professional organization and contact them. In my experience therapists contacted in this way are very helpful because they are not worried that you are going to steal their clients.

- ☐ Where your professional organization has local group meetings, go along and speak to as many people as possible. For example, the Association of Reflexologists has local group meetings throughout the country. At the meeting you will get to meet a wide variety of therapists. Some will be earning their living from their therapies, some will be working part-time to fit in with other commitments and some will just be carrying out the odd treatment because they love the therapy. By meeting fellow therapists in this way you can find out far more than you could on the phone.

☐ Limited companies have to file their accounts annually and, for a small fee, you can download from the Companies House website financial information about a particular company. This doesn't give you the whole picture, but it can give you an indication of how well the business is performing.

☐ You can ring up local practitioners and ask them how soon they can fit you in for a treatment. This will give you an idea of how busy they are.

 When you first start your practice and have few clients, if a prospective client rings you up and asks for an appointment, find out when would be convenient for them before offering them an appointment. If you say they can come any time, this tells them you are not busy and they may decide to go for a therapist who is more in demand.

QUESTIONS TO ASK PRACTISING THERAPISTS

Before you contact any therapists you should decide the questions you need to ask. This will avoid you having to go back to them at a later date if you haven't collected all the information you need. You can base your questions on the following list:

☐ How long have you been practising?

☐ How long did it take you to build up your business to what it is now?

☐ How many appointment slots do you have each week?

☐ How many clients do you normally treat each week?

☐ Where do you work (including multiple locations)?

☐ Is there any seasonal variation in your appointments?

☐ How much do you charge?

☐ How long are your sessions?

☐ How do you market your services?

☐ What is the best method you have found of finding new clients?

☐ If you were starting again from scratch as a therapist, what would you do differently?

☐ What advice do you have for me as a new therapist?

Exercise

Using the methods above, make an estimate of the number of treatments you should expect to be carrying out each month once you are established. Do the same for any product you will be selling.

Once I am established:

☐ My maximum number of client appointments each week is:

....

☐ I expect to sell this number of products each week:

....

Building up your clients

You have predicted the maximum number of treatments you will be able to carry out each month, now you need to think about how those client numbers will build up. With the greatest will in the world you won't suddenly start on day one with a full clinic. You will need to build up your client base, and how quickly this happens is up to you. The more marketing you do the faster you will build up your client base. For your financial forecasts you can assume you will find your clients gradually, or you can look back at your marketing plan and work out when you are likely to find the most clients.

Don't assume that you will pick up clients straight after each marketing event you carry out. I always ask new clients where they found my details or heard about me. When I asked a new client this question one day I was told that she had attended a talk I had given on reflexology nearly 18 months before!

Exercise

In the previous exercise you estimated how many treatments you would be carrying out when you were established. Enter that number in the table below at month 12. Then fill in the table for previous months, either assuming that new clients will come to you in a predictable manner or basing this information on your marketing plan. Do the same with secondary treatments and any product you plan to sell.

For this exercise a spreadsheet is by far the easiest option, but you can use a table and (later) a calculator.

Month	1	2	3	4	5	6	7	8	9	10	11	12
Treatment 1												
Treatment 2												
Product 1												
Product 2												

Is your business seasonal?

Most therapists will notice some seasonal variation in the number of their clients. As I have said before, I find August is generally slow because many clients are on holiday and January is also slow because many clients are still paying for Christmas. However, a therapist who also sold jewellery might find that they do more business in December, because of clients buying gifts for family and friends, than they do in the whole of the rest of the year.

Exercise

Look at the information in the previous exercise. Instead of looking at month 1, month 2 etc., enter the names of the months onto the table, and then make adjustments to your figures based on any seasonal variations you expect to find.

Month	January	February	March	April	May	June	July	August	September	October	November	December
Treatment 1												
Treatment 2												
Product 1												
Product 2												

When will I make money?

As the owner of your business you will need to know when you are going to start making a profit. So add to your table the revenue you will receive from your treatments, your fixed costs, split between each month (start by splitting this amount equally between each month) and your capital costs, which again initially can be split equally between the first 12 months.

EXAMPLE ONE

Sally is setting up as a therapist and will work part-time from home. Once she is established she hopes to complete 35 treatments each month and she will charge £30 per treatment. Sally has kept her costs low and has estimated that her fixed costs are £1,253 each year and her initial set-up costs are £680. Each treatment she gives will cost her £2.45 in terms of consumables and washing. Sally is hoping to earn £700 each month.

Looking at the spreadsheet opposite, if Sally spreads her fixed and set-up costs over the year, she is just about making a profit from month 1, although she doesn't start earning the £700 a month she wants until November. However, this doesn't last and because Sally expects December to be a quiet month, she falls below her £700 income.

Sally

Month	January	February	March	April	May	June	July	August	September	October	November	December
Treatments	6	10	14	18	20	22	22	20	28	31	33	28
Treatment revenue at £30	£180	£300	£420	£540	£600	£660	£660	£600	£840	£930	£990	£840
Fixed costs per month	£161	£161	£161	£161	£161	£161	£161	£161	£161	£161	£161	£161
Variable costs per treatment at £2.45	£15	£25	£34	£44	£49	£54	£54	£49	£69	£76	£81	£69
Total of fixed and variable costs	£176	£186	£195	£205	£210	£215	£215	£210	£230	£237	£242	£230
Profit	£4	£114	£225	£335	£390	£445	£445	£390	£610	£693	£748	£610

EXAMPLE TWO

Now let's look at Peter. Although initially his costs are very similar to Sally's, with fixed costs of £1,226 each year, Peter needs to earn £2,000 each month. He works out that to achieve this he will need to hire premises, so initially he hires a room for four days a week at a cost of £52 a day, and works at his home treatment room on the fifth day. Peter has now increased his running costs by £204 a week but his set-up costs have also increased to £960 because he has to buy duplicates of some of his equipment to leave at the room he is renting.

Peter has researched his clients and found that he should maximize the number of his client by offering 30-minute treatments, for which he believes he can charge £25.

From Peter's spreadsheet opposite we can see that, he will make a loss during his first month and won't earn his required £2,000 until September, unless he increases his marketing campaign and so find clients sooner, or reduces his costs.

Exercise

For your prospective business, take the information you have compiled in the above exercises and expand it to produce a projection of your profit for the next 12 months.

Month	January	February	March	April	May	June	July	August	September	October	November	December
Treatments												
Treatment revenue												
Revenue from products												
Total revenue												
Fixed costs per month												
Variable costs per treatment												
Total cost												
Profit												

Peter

Month	January	February	March	April	May	June	July	August	September	October	November	December
Treatments	20	40	60	80	100	120	120	100	150	160	170	160
Treatment revenue at £25	£500	£1,000	£1,500	£2,000	£2,500	£3,000	£3,000	£2,500	£3,750	£4,000	£4,250	£4,000
Fixed costs per month	£182	£182	£182	£182	£182	£182	£182	£182	£182	£182	£182	£182
Location costs	£901	£901	£901	£901	£901	£901	£901	£901	£901	£901	£901	£901
Variable costs per treatment at £2.45	£49	£98	£147	£196	£245	£294	£294	£245	£368	£392	£417	£392
Total of fixed and variable costs	£1,133	£1,182	£1,231	£1,280	£1,329	£1,378	£1,378	£1,329	£1,451	£1,476	£1,500	£1,476
Profit	–£633	–£182	£270	£721	£1,172	£1,623	£1,623	£1,172	£2,299	£2,525	£2,750	£2,525

Changing your projections

If you have spoken to other therapists and completed your research, your figures should be realistic but you are never going to get them exactly right. What you can do to minimize your risk is take the projection you have produced above, copy it and produce two more projections, the first one more optimistic than your original and the second more pessimistic.

But what if your projections are not forecasting the profit you want? In that case you have two choices: increase your predicted number of clients or reduce your costs.

To increase your predicted number of clients you will need to boost the amount of marketing you are planning. You can also increase client numbers with special offers, although remember that if you do this you will erode your profit per client.

Be careful about reducing your costs because you want to cut costs only in those areas that won't affect your long-term profitability. Let's look again at the figures for Peter. One way he could reduce costs would be to start by renting his room only on one day a week, building to four days a week by the end of his first year in business.

By building up his costs gradually, Peter manages to make a small profit in January and by June is making his required £2,000 a month. Peter still has the option of increasing his marketing effort to bring in clients sooner, which has not been reflected in this spreadsheet.

Exercise

If I needed to reduce my costs, I could consider the following:

1.

....

2.

....

3.

....

Peter with reduced rent

Month	January	February	March	April	May	June	July	August	September	October	November	December
Treatments	20	40	60	80	100	120	120	100	150	160	170	160
Treatment revenue at £25	£500	£1,000	£1,500	£2,000	£2,500	£3,000	£3,000	£2,500	£3,750	£4,000	£4,250	£4,000
Fixed costs per month	£182	£182	£182	£182	£182	£182	£182	£182	£182	£182	£182	£182
Location costs	£225	£225	£225	£451	£451	£451	£676	£676	£676	£901	£901	£901
Variable costs per treatment at £2.45	£49	£98	£147	£196	£245	£294	£294	£245	£368	£392	£417	£392
Total of fixed and variable costs	£457	£506	£555	£829	£878	£927	£1,152	£1,103	£1,226	£1,476	£1,500	£1,476
Profit	£44	£495	£946	£1,171	£1,622	£2,073	£1,848	£1,397	£2,524	£2,525	£2,750	£2,525

If I needed to attract more clients I could:

1.

....

2.

....

3.

....

Should I be VAT registered?

If your turnover (i.e. all the money you receive into your business) is above £70,000 (this figure is valid for 2011) then you need to register for VAT. However, even if your turnover is less than the specified amount you can choose to be VAT registered.

Once you are registered for VAT you have to charge VAT at the current rate on all of your sales of services or products. The rate is now 20% (2011), so for all of your clients this is effectively increasing your prices by 20%. So, if you currently charge £50 for a treatment, once you have added VAT on to the price of the treatment you will be charging £60. This could make your service less competitive, leading to fewer clients and therefore less profit.

The advantage to being registered for VAT is that you can claim back the VAT on all the supplies you buy. So, for example, if in a year you spend £900 on VAT-registered supplies, and the VAT is 20%, the goods would have been priced at (£900 × 100)/120 which equals £750. So, if you were VAT registered you would be able to claim £900 minus £750, which equals £150.

Remember, the VAT threshold is based on your *turnover*, that is, all the money you receive for services and products; it does not depend at all on your *profit*.

You need to ask yourself the following question: 'Is the money I receive back from the VAT man worth the loss of competitive advantage caused by having to put up my prices?'

Exercise

Imagine you are VAT registered.

Work out how much your treatments will cost with VAT added.

....

Go back to your competitor analysis. Would this increase in price affect how competitive you are?

....

Work out how much you spend on VAT, registered supplies.

....

Given the choice, which is only yours if your turnover is less than £68,000, should you be registered for VAT?

....

10
RUNNING YOUR BUSINESS

This chapter looks at your business plan, where you can go for business advice, the records you need to keep, the advantages of having an accountant, the options involved when you are taking payments, and whether or not you need a business bank account.

Drawing up your business plan

A business plan is a description of your business, what you are planning to do, how you are planning to market your business and how much money you expect to make.

A business plan is essential if you need to borrow money to set up or run your business. It shows potential lenders or investors that you know what you are doing, have considered your options and have a good understanding of what makes a profitable business.

It is also essential if you are setting up your business as a partnership, or a limited company with more than one director. You can then be sure that everyone involved is aware of how you are going to move the business foreward and they can give their agreement.

Even if you don't need external finance to set up your business, a business plan can still help you, as the business owner, to make your business as successful as you want it to be. It can help you spot potential problems before they occur. For example, if you need to earn £50,000k a year from your therapies, your business plan may show that to do this you would need to work 90 hours a week. A business plan is also a kind of snapshot of your business, so that in the future you can look back and measure how far you have come from your first tentative steps into business.

WHAT TO INCLUDE IN YOUR PLAN

Business plans come in a multitude of formats and designs, but a simple one could include an executive summary, details of the people who are going to make your business happen, a description of the business, a marketing plan and financial forecasts. The following list is a guide to what to include.

1. Executive Summary. This is a brief summary of your business and how you see it working.

2. People. List who will be involved in your business and how the business will be set up. For example, you may be the only person in your business and you may be self-employed or a limited company. Your business could be set up as a partnership, or a limited company with several directors. You could be planning to involve any number of other therapists or administration staff, permanently or on an ad hoc basis.

3. Description of your business. Detail what therapies and products you will be offering in year 1. Describe the premises you will be treating from and what hours you will be working.

4. Marketing:

   ☐ Clients – describe who you think your clients will be and how you are going to sell to them.

   ☐ Competitors – include a list of your competitors, with the analysis you performed on them.

5. Financial forecasts. State your expected costs, your expected income and, from those figures, the profit you expect to make from your business.

Exercise

We have already covered most of the items within your business plan in previous exercises, so put all the information together to create your own business plan.

Where can I go for business advice?

Many organizations offer advice and guidance to new businesses. These include banks and local business support groups such as Business Link. Business Link is a government-funded agency so most of the services it offers are free to local businesses. They can be found at www.businesslink.gov.uk.

What records do I need to keep?

If you are going to work as a self-employed therapist, in a partnership or as a limited company, you need to keep good financial records. This is not only to ensure you pay the correct amount of tax and National Insurance but also so that you can accurately calculate the profit your business is making each year and so make the right decisions for your business. For example, to keep your business profitable you may need to increase your prices or reduce your costs. You will only know this if you keep accurate records.

It is a Financial Services Authority (FSA) requirement that records are kept for **seven years** including the current tax year.

Records should include:

☐ all income received (i.e. payments from clients);

☐ all business expenses;

☐ drawings for self (i.e. money you are taking out of the business as wages);

☐ loans or other finance put into the business.

If you are an employee you should also keep records of all of your expenses. Even though you are employed you may be required to pay your own therapy organization membership (such as the Association of Reflexologists (AoR) or Federation of Holistic Therapists (FHT)), your own insurance and subscriptions and to provide your own tools or specialist uniform. If you have to use your car for business and your employer does not pay your mileage, or only pays you a reduced rate, you may also be able to claim for this, although not for your normal commute to work.

Exercise

Make a list of the expenses you expect to pay and split them into three sections: one-off set-up costs; annual costs, such as the membership of your professional organization and your insurance costs; and other costs which directly relate to the number of clients you treat. For example, if you buy couch roll, the more people you treat, the more rolls you will have to buy.

WHAT INFORMATION TO KEEP

You will have to prove that the figures in your accounts for expenses and income are genuine. You should keep:

☐ chequebook stubs and any cancelled cheques;

☐ bank statements and paying in books;

☐ copies of your invoices;

☐ supplier invoices, all receipts and delivery notes.

HOW TO DOCUMENT INCOME AND EXPENDITURE

You have three options when documenting your income and expenditure.

1. Keep your records manually, using a specialist accounts book from a stationer's, or you can do it completely from scratch, starting with a blank sheet of paper, although this is not the easiest method.

2. Use a spreadsheet. This has the advantage that all the adding up is done for you and it is easy to cross-check your figures.

3. Buy an accounting package, such as Sage Instant Accounts, TAS Books, Intuit QuickBooks and QuickBooks Pro, Regular and Accountant, or Pegasus Capital Gold. However, if you are also using an accountant, make sure your system is compatible with theirs.

Generally speaking, if you are going to work as a self-employed therapist, I would advise the spreadsheet option. If you are setting up a clinic, where you will be employing other therapists or they will be working for you on a self-employed basis, I would use an accounting package. In either case, if your turnover is over £70,000, you will need to be VAT registered so, with that added complication, I would again go for a package.

SIMPLE SPREADSHEET OPTION

If you are going for a simple spreadsheet you will need four sheets, one each for income, expenses, drawings, and the final sheet for any money you put into the business.

Income

You should record all of your income on this page. Include:

☐ the date the payment was made;

☐ who made the payment;

☐ what the payment was for (if you offer more than one therapy or service);

☐ how the payment was made (e.g., cash, cheque, bank transfer, credit card);

☐ the amount paid.

Expenses

You should record all of your expenses, making sure that everything you record is an allowable expense (that is, it is necessary in order for you to do your job).

Make a note of:

- [ ] the date the invoice was received;

- [ ] the supplier's name;

- [ ] the supplier's reference number (if applicable);

- [ ] the amount paid;

- [ ] the date the payment was made.

Don't forget to include expenses like bank charges that are deducted directly from your bank account and any standing orders or direct debits. You also need to include an amount for any utility bills, such as electricity, gas, water and telephone, that are split between your business and your home.

I also like to include an additional field called 'type'. This allows me to work out more easily where I am spending my money. So, for example, all my costs to do with my professional qualification, such as membership of the AoR and insurance, are marked as 'AoR'. All my consumables, such as creams, foot cleansers and couch roll, go under 'consumables'. All my stationery goes under 'stationery', and all my computing costs, including virus checker renewal and firewalls, backup discs and maintenance, go under 'computer'. You don't need to do this but I find it helps me.

Drawings

You need to document your drawings or wages. This can be achieved simply by keeping track of:

- [ ] the date you took the money out of the business;

- [ ] the amount of money withdrawn;

- [ ] how the transfer took place (e.g., cheque, bank transfer, etc.).

You can also use this sheet to document your National Insurance payments, and to work out your tax liability. You are allowed to earn £6,475 (tax year 2010/11) before you have to pay tax, which works out at just under £540 a month. So if you are paying yourself more than £540 a month you must ensure that you reserve the tax you will need to pay to the Inland Revenue and don't spend it.

Money put into the business

If you have put any money into your business, or have taken out a loan, either in the business's name or for the benefit of the business, this must be included on the final page of your spreadsheet. Interest and other charges on business loans should also be included on your expenses page.

> *The first year I ran my business I wasn't very organized. I put all my receipts into a box and at the end of the year it took me ages to transfer that information to a spreadsheet. I also found that I couldn't read some of the older receipts very well, and I'm sure that because of this I had valid business expenses which I couldn't claim for. I have now devised a system. I still put my receipts into a box, but each month I transfer the details to my spreadsheet. Also, if the receipt looks as if it might fade, I write on it what it was for and the amount. If I have any mileage to claim associated with the receipt, I also write this on it, so that I don't miss anything. Sometimes I buy items for my business when I'm doing my family shopping. If I do this I generally try to get a separate receipt – so, if you see somebody going round the supermarket with a basket inside a trolley, it might be me! If I'm only buying one or two items for myself, I cross these personal items off the receipt and recalculate the total before I file it.*

CAPITAL EXPENSES

Some of your expenses, especially your set-up expenses, will need to be handled slightly differently from everyday expenses. Capital expenditure is basically for anything that will last the business for more than one year and is an asset of the business. So, if you need to buy a couch, tools, a chair, desk, computer, a desk for your home office, or a printer, these are all items that will last several years and so are treated as an asset to your business.

The way capital expenses are handled changed in 2008. Now, capital expenses up to £50,000 can be claimed each year in a similar way to everyday expenses. However, they need to be documented separately, because if you sell any asset once you have claimed tax relief on it, the amount you sell the item for needs to be added to your turnover.

Example

When you set up your business you bought a couch for £180 to carry out your treatments and you claimed for the couch in your Annual Investment Allowance (AIA). After working with the couch for a year, you find you really need a more robust electric couch and purchase one for £800. You no longer need your original couch and sell it for £70. This £70 then becomes income to your business.

BUSINESS USE OF YOUR CAR

If you use your car for your business you have two options:

1. You can work out your total car expenses and then claim a percentage for business use based on mileage;

2. You can claim a mileage rate of 40p a mile (2011 rate) from HM Revenue and Customs.

In the first option you work out all of the expenses associated with your car and divide them up based on your actual mileage. So, if your car costs you £3,000 during one year, and in that year you drive 5,000 business miles and 5,000 personal miles, you can claim for half of your £3,000 costs. If you don't do many miles, it is normally more cost-effective and easier to claim a mileage rate which covers both the fuel and maintenance of your car. This is currently 40p per mile for the first 10,000 business miles and 25p per mile for any further mileage (this amount is valid for 2011).

Remember that if you do use your car for business you will need to inform your car insurance provider and ensure your business mileage is covered.

Do I need an accountant?

This depends totally on you and how good you are with figures. If you start your business as self-employed, you have to keep a record of all your earnings and expenses and complete a tax return each year. If your turnover (i.e. the money that comes into your business) is over £70,000 you will also have to complete a VAT return. Many self-employed therapists do this with no problem. The advantage of using an accountant is that because they know exactly what business expenses are acceptable, they can ensure you claim everything possible against your income. Many accountants offer a free introductory session where they look at your finances and offer advice. It is worth booking one of these.

If you have set yourself up as a limited company, you have to submit accounts at the right time and in the correct format. Again, it is perfectly possible to do this yourself, but if you are new to business I would recommend you employ the services of an accountant.

The golden rule is that the accountant should be able to show that the fees they charge you are more than covered by the tax savings they show to you.

> ' *Val is a great therapist but money is not her strong point. During her first year she collected all her receipts and kept them in a big box. At the end of the year, when it came for her to fill in her tax 'returns', she felt totally out of her depth so an accountant friend stepped in to help. Although Val had kept all the receipts for everything she had bought to carry out her therapy, she was missing receipts for a lot of items she could claim for. For example, she regularly attended training courses, and although she had included receipts for the cost of the training courses, she didn't include any for travel to or from the venues, overnight accommodation, meals or any additional books or tools she purchased during the courses. Her accountant gave her a list of the things she could claim for, so she is now much better at*  *writing everything down, but at the end of the tax year she still hands her accountant a box full of receipts. Val knows that the accountant is charging her more than if she gave him the receipt details on a spreadsheet, but she is not very computer literate so she is happy with that. She also knows she doesn't have the advantage of being able to monitor her business month by month, but as she now has a fairly stable clientele, this is not an aspect which worries her.* '

Providing Information

Although for all of your expenses you need to keep a number of documents to prove you have incurred the cost, such as receipts, bank statements, etc., when you complete your accounts or fill in your annual tax return, if you are self-employed, you only have to provide summary information.

Example

If you are self-employed, you will need to provide the following information each year:

- ☐ **Turnover:** This is your income (not profit), which includes all revenue from treatments, selling products, and any tips or other payments in kind.

- ☐ **Expenses:** This includes the cost of any products you use, use of your car for business, business use of your home (heat and light) to carry out your treatments or for you to use as an office, membership of professional organizations, insurance, etc.

- ☐ **AIA:** You need to document anything you are claiming for under your Annual Investment Allowance. So, looking at your capital expenses, such as equipment, tools, computers, office desk, you can claim up to a maximum of £50,000 each year against your tax. More details are on the HMRC website at www.hmrc.gov.uk.

- ☐ **Capital expenses:** If your capital expenses in any one year are more than £50,000, the excess can be claimed as capital expenses, generally at 20% of the value of the item each year. Some businesses choose to account for their assets using capital expenses rather than the Annual Investment Allowance.

How do I take payments from clients?

For many therapists, having carried out case studies as part of their training, where they treat clients for nothing, starting to take money can be daunting. It can bring up all sorts of insecurities about being good enough or giving value for money. Other therapists can't wait to start earning their living doing something they love, so taking payment can't come too soon.

One way of easing your case study clients into paying, once you have qualified, is to send them all a letter thanking them for their support during your training and enclosing a voucher for money off their next treatment. If you are in the 'can't get started soon enough' camp, make the voucher valid for 10% or 20% off, as this is still a great marketing tool. If you are in the 'I'm worried about charging' camp, give them a whopping 50% off. Either way you are letting your clients know you are ready to start your business and giving them an incentive to come to see you. For some therapies, you might also consider enclosing a few vouchers that they can pass on to their friends. Don't forget to specify that the vouchers cannot be used by existing clients and put a 'use by date' on the voucher, as you don't want to be giving big discounts once you are busy.

When you are thinking about how to take payment, consider the advantages and disadvantages of:

☐ cash;

☐ cheque;

☐ standing order;

☐ credit card;

☐ debit card.

CASH

The main advantages of cash are that it can be spent straight away, it can't bounce, and taking cash doesn't cost you any money.

The disadvantages include:

☐ Cash on the premises could be a security issue.

☐ Cash is too easy to spend. Remember that from the money you receive for your treatments you need to set aside enough for all of your costs and expenses, and to pay your tax and NI contributions.

☐ There is no record to show whether or not a client has paid.

☐ You need to ensure you have change readily available.

☐ If you take a lot of cash you will need to visit the bank regularly to pay in. This is time when you are not available to give treatments.

CHEQUE

Although the banks are trying to discourage the use of cheques, they are a convenient method of payment for many people.

The advantages of cheques include:

☐ There is no cash lying around.

☐ It's easy for you to keep your books.

☐ You have proof of payment.

☐ Cheques can be written in advance.

☐ No change is needed.

The disadvantages of using cheques include:

☐ They may limit cash-in-hand/petty cash.

☐ You may incur bank charges when paying cheques into your account.

☐ Cheques need time to clear before money can be spent or bills paid.

☐ Cheques may bounce, which could mean you incur bank charges.

☐ The use of cheques is being discouraged by the banks and they will be withdrawn at some point.

STANDING ORDER

Standing orders are very easy to account for, there can be no debate about whether or not a client has paid and, once set up, a standing order is automatic and promotes customer loyalty. The problem with standing orders is that clients may be resistant to committing to them and, on your side, it requires good organizational skills to ensure a client's treatments are registered as taken.

❝ *Bea runs a clinic with her husband Michael and between them they offer a variety of treatments. They offer incentives to encourage clients to choose how many treatments they wish to commit to, and then to set up a standing order to pay for their treatments. Firstly, the client will receive some free treatments. For example, if they pay for 12 treatments in a year they will be able to take 15. Secondly, Bea and Michael have guaranteed that the cost of their treatments will always be less than for those clients paying on the day. For example, if the standard price of a treatment is £22, clients with standing orders will only pay £20. Additionally, to make the package more flexible, clients can give their treatment vouchers as gifts to their friends and family members.* ❞

CREDIT CARD

Lots of people use their credit cards to pay for almost everything they buy, so many clients will expect you to be able to take payment this way. This can also attract customers who do not have money readily to hand in the bank. With credit cards you don't have the problems associated with cash or cheques; a credit card payment is proof of payment and you don't need to visit the bank to get your money. However, taking credit cards is expensive. You will have to pay a monthly fee for hire of the streamer, as well  as a percentage of all the monies taken. There is also the problem that if the credit card has been used fraudulently, you may lose all or some of the payment.

DEBIT CARD

Many people use their debit card in the same way as a credit card and to you it has the same advantages. Cost of usage is again a disadvantage because you still have to pay a monthly fee for hire of the streamer, although with debit cards there are not normally any additional fees.

> *Harjit runs an acupuncture clinic and because of the cost of the treatments he is offering he decided he needed to be able to accept payment by card. But to reduce his costs, he encourages all of his clients to pay by debit card rather than credit card, which is slightly cheaper for him. Harjit no longer accepts cheques so the cost of processing the cards is slightly offset by the fact that he no longer has to spend time visiting his bank.*

TIP If you don't accept payment by card, ensure that when a client books a treatment with you they know how they can pay. If you forget and the client doesn't have cash or cheques with them, they can find it so embarrassing that they can be put off visiting you again.

Do I need a business bank account?

Generally the problem with business bank accounts is that after an initial one-year or 18-month period of free banking, you will have to pay bank charges. This is at a time when, if you are in credit, most personal accounts don't incur charges. So, do you need a business account?

If you set up as self-employed you definitely need a separate account because it is important to keep your personal finances separate from your business finances. However, because of the bank charges many people start with a personal account, which means they don't pay charges. But this is not something that banks encourage and if they discover you are using a personal account for business, they could backdate the business rate charges.

If you set up in a partnership or a limited company then you will definitely need to start with a business account.

11
YOUR SET-UP ACTION PLAN

Setting up any new business is an immense task; it can seem so daunting that it is hard to know where to begin. But the key is to do *something*. Make a list of everything you are going to do for your business. Include even tiny things because you don't want to forget anything and it is so nice to cross them off your list. This list is in addition to your marketing plan.

Getting started

Your action list might include the following:

- ☐ Set up your company (register as self-employed, set up a limited company, etc.);

- ☐ Set up a bank account.

- ☐ Order a credit/debit card streamer.

- ☐ Order any additional equipment you require to carry out your treatments.

- ☐ Obtain a stock of the consumables you will be using (e.g. couch roll).

- ☐ Make your treatment room or clinic ready.

- ☐ Investigate working at additional clinics on different days of the week.

- ☐ Buy your uniforms.

- ☐ Find an accountant. If you are going to use an accountant they can make sure you keep all of your financial information in a format which will minimize work for you later on.

- ☐ Interview and employ any staff you need.

- ☐ Buy cash books or set up a spreadsheet to allow you to keep track of your incoming and outgoing money.

- ☐ Arrange your insurance:

    - ☐ Ensure your car insurance covers you for business use.

    - ☐ Check your house insurance if you are working at home.

☐ Obtain insurance for your clinic.

☐ Investigate other insurance policies, e.g. cover for your equipment, cover in case you cannot work because of illness, health insurance.

☐ Obtain a system for keeping track of clients. This can be a diary and a filing cabinet if you are working on your own or a full computerized appointments system if you are running a clinic.

☐ Contact Business Link for a free discussion about your plans.

☐ Investigate any grants available for new businesses in your area.

Any big steps can be split into separate smaller ones. For example, 'Set up a bank account' could be split into three steps:

1. Research different accounts, including charges, charge-free periods, which can range from 12 months to two years, and location of the nearest branch if you have to visit the bank to pay in cash or cheques.

2. Choose which bank account will be best/cheapest for you. This is not always easy because when you start you don't know how many cheques you will need to pay in relative to the amount of money which will be paid by bank transfer, and each bank seems to charge for its services in a different way.

3. Open the account and complete all the paperwork.

You can mark each item with a priority. As I said in Chapter 6, talking about marketing plans, when you are running your own business you never have enough time. By looking at each item and deciding if it is a high, medium or low priority, you can ensure that anything you don't get around to falls into the low priority category.

If you wish you can also mark each item with both the time you estimate it will take to complete and an approximate start and finish date. For example, although opening a bank account should be very simple, I would allow three weeks for the action to be accomplished because once you have completed your paperwork the bank will need a couple of weeks to carry out its administration tasks. So, although it may only take a couple of hours of your time, the start and end dates should be at least three weeks apart.

As you complete each action you can cross it off your list – very satisfying.

So the process is:

1. Make a list of all the things you need to do;

2. Assign a priority to each item, high, medium or low;

3. Estimate how long each task will take;

4. Give each item a start and finish date;

5. Cross each item off as you complete it.

This is my action plan:

Item	Description	Time	H/M/L	Start date	End date
1					
2					
3					
4					
5					
6					
7					
8					
9					
10					

Staying SMART

Make sure your actions are all SMART

S   Specific

M   Measurable

A   Achievable

R   Realistic

T   Time related

12
AND FINALLY

In the previous chapters we have looked at each separate area involved in starting a business. When you come to set up your own business, you will need to give each of the areas equal consideration. It is no good thinking up a brilliant name for your business if you haven't decided which therapies you are going to offer. Nor is there any point in renting a streamer to take credit card payments if you haven't promoted your services and so don't have any clients.

If you have followed the guidance in this book step by step you should have drawn up the following documents:

Business Plan
This document describes your business and your services and includes financial projections which will help to show you both what you want for your new business and that what you want is achievable.

Set-up Action Plan
This document should take you step by step through the actions you need to complete in order to get your business up and running.

Promotion Plan
This document describes the initial actions you have decided to take to promote your new therapy business.

Marketing Plans
These documents will remind you of what you need to do regularly to remain competitive in the marketplace and to ensure that you run enough promotional activities to provide you with a continuous steady flow of clients, not just when you are building up your clients as you start your business.

With these documents you have all the information you need to start your business. I would like to wish you luck and hope you find your journey as a therapist as satisfying as I have found mine. Finally, let me pass on some inspiring words from the great German writer, Goethe (1749–1832):

> Whatever you can do, or dream you can, begin it.
> Boldness has genius, power and magic in it.

ADDITIONAL INFORMATION SHEET 1

This is an evaluation list and should be used for all leaflets, posters, advertisements and any other printed material you are producing to promote your business.

1. Who is your promotional material aimed at?

2. What message is it trying to give to the reader?

3. What does it ask the reader to do?

4. What does the quality of the paper tell you?

5. What does its colour tell you?

6. Does it look professional?

7. Does it look too cheap or too expensive?

8. Are the contact details clear?

9. Does it contain any spelling mistakes?

10. Is the formatting correct?

11. Does the reader need any prior knowledge to understand the advertisement or does it contain all the information they need?

12. Read the advertisement out loud. Does it make sense?

13. Read the advertisement again. Is there anything missing?

14. Does the advertisement contain anything that may offend anybody at all?

15. Does the advertisement contain anything that readers may misunderstand?

16. What would you do if you received this advertisement from somebody else?

17. If this is an advertisement to be printed in a publication, will it stand out? Make a copy of the advertisement the correct size and stick it into your chosen publication. Can you see it? How does it look against the other advertisements?

18. What do your friends/colleagues think of this advertisement?

ADDITIONAL INFORMATION SHEET 2

LETTER TO PTA PROPOSING A 'LADIES EVENING' FUND-RAISING EVENT

Your address,

Your town,

Your county,

Your postcode

Tel: Your telephone number

Email: Your email

www.yourwebsite

PTA Chairman's Name

Parent Teacher Association,

C/o Name of school,

Address of school,

Town

County

Date

Dear Name,

<u>Fund-raising event</u>

I am writing to enquire whether you run or would be interested in running a 'ladies' evening' to raise funds for your school. These events can be staged in the evening or during the weekend and can be a mixture of exhibitors selling products, therapists offering taster treatments, and talks and demonstrations. Entry to the event is normally by ticket and, to encourage people to attend, the ticket can entitle the bearer to a drink and a small snack.

Exhibitors selling products would pay for their display area and the money would go directly to school funds. Therapists offering taster treatments can either pay for their stand, in which case they keep the money raised from their taster treatments, or they don't pay for their stand but donate a percentage of the profit from the taster treatments they carry out. Additionally all exhibitors can be asked to donate a raffle prize, which further raises funds for the school. These events can also work as mother and daughter events.

If you are interested in arranging a ladies' evening, or a mother and daughter evening, I would happily attend as a therapist offering taster treatments/give a talk on my therapy/exhibit and sell Product X.

Please contact me if you would like more information.

Yours sincerely,

Name

ADDITIONAL INFORMATION SHEET 3

TASTER TREATMENT BOOKING FORM

If I am busy and you would like a treatment please enter your name below and return at the stated time.

Time	Name	Payment
10.30		
10.45		
11.00		
11.15		
11.30		
11.45		
12.00		
12.15		
12.30		
12.45		
1.00		
1.15		

Please ensure you have completed a consultation form before you return at your allotted time.

Thanks, Jackie

ADDITIONAL INFORMATION SHEET 4

MEDICAL QUESTIONNAIRE

Please complete this form before your treatment start time.

Name: Address:

Tel:

Mobile:

Email:

GP Name: GP Address:

GP Telephone number:

Date of birth: /   /   Sex: M/F   Are you Pregnant? Y/N/n.a.

Do you or have you suffered from any of the following:

List all the contraindications to your therapy.

Are you currently suffering from:

Pain ☐   Inflammation ☐   Any infectious disease ☐

Are you currently receiving, or have you recently received,
any medical treatment?   Y/N

Are you scheduled for any medical tests or procedures
in the future?   Y/N

Are you taking any medication?   Y/N

Are you under the care of a specialist doctor?   Y/N

Are you currently seeing a complementary therapist?

Do you have any allergies?   Y/N

Please specify any problems with any particular area covered by your therapy.

Please list any serious illnesses and injuries you have suffered from, giving dates.

Additional information:

I have been informed about the treatment and agree to accept a treatment.

Date: /   /   **Signed:** ....

USEFUL WEBSITES
(All websites current at 1 November 2010)

Therapist sites

www.ctha.com: Complementary Therapists Association.

www.fht.org.uk: Federation of Holistic Therapists. They claim to be the UK's largest organization of professional therapists.

www.nhsdirectory.org: This is a directory of complementary therapies and therapists. It is fairly new at the moment so doesn't have too many therapists listed, but depending on the therapies offered it may well be worth therapists paying for a listing.

Commercial therapist listings sites

www.embodyforyou.com: This also claims to be the UK's largest organization of professional therapists. However, it includes beauty therapists.

www.chisuk.org.uk: This is a commercial listings site.

www.worldwidehealth.com: This is another commercial listings site.

Commercial business listings sites

www.touchlocal.co.uk: Business listings directory. It is a commercial site but it is free to add your business.

www.yell.com: Again you can add a free listing.

Government sites

www.businesslink.gov.uk: A government organization that offers free business advice and training.

www.hmrc.gov.uk/index.htm: HM Revenue and Customs site, for queries on tax, National Insurance, pensions and VAT.

www.direct.gov.uk/en/index.htm: Lots of information including advice about pensions.

www.companieshouse.gov.uk/: Information on limited companies.

www.hse.gov.uk/: Information on health and safety matters.

Internet

www.123-reg.co.uk/: Use this site to set up web addresses or check the availability of the address you want.

Miscellaneous

www.macmillan.org.uk/Cancerinformation/Cancertreatment/Complementary therapies/Complementarytherapies.aspx: This site looks at the use of complementary therapies to help cancer suffers. It can be useful to use sites like these when designing your marketing.

INDEX

Some other titles from How To Books

MARKETING YOUR COMPLEMENTARY THERAPY PRACTICE
101 tried and tested ways to attract and retain clients

Steven A Harold

'If you are serious about being a professional Complementary Therapist then get yourself a copy of this book now.' LINDA STEWART, www.holistic-business.com

'Being in business all my adult life, both practising and teaching, I thought I knew it all. Reading this book woke me up.' INTERNATIONAL THERAPIST

If you use this book as it is intended you should be able to create a tidal wave of enquiries from potential clients, you can then let your therapy skills take over.

ISBN 978-1-84528-449-7

HOW TO FRANCHISE YOUR BUSINESS
Grow your business by creating and managing a franchised network.

Brian Duckett and Paul Monaghan

If you have a proven business system and are wishing to expand, franchising is a strong option. It provides a quick route to growth and uses other people's money and enthusiasm to open individual offices, shops, restaurants, salons, surgeries, units, van rounds, or service centres. This book provides practical advice on how franchising works from two authors with years of experience. As well as being for potential franchisors, this book is also invaluable to owners of existing branch networks, practising franchisors and their management teams, and candidates for the Diploma in Franchise Management.

ISBN 978-1-84528-476-3

START AND RUN A BUSINESS FROM HOME
Plus 10 great businesses that you can run from home

Paul Power

This book will show you how to turn your passion and enthusiasm into a viable business. It is packed full of practical, down-to-earth advice based on the author's own, and other successful entrepreneurs', experience. Discover how you can easily research your ideas, start your own business at home, from little or nothing and market your business on a shoestring.

'His no-nonsense approach is inspirational.' *Goodtimes*

ISBN 978-1-84528-301-8

A PRACTICAL GUIDE TO MENTORING
Down to earth guidance on making mentoring work for you

David Kay and Roger Hinds

'As a ready reference and guidance note, this publication fits the bill. … a sound investment. I particularly liked the mentoring scenarios which give a flavour of the types of issues that may arise.' TRAINING JOURNAL

Mentoring is a rewarding experience. You will play an active and invaluable part in the development of another person and further your own career at the same time.

This concise book will take you step-by-step through the process and clarify the whole mentoring process from start to finish.

ISBN 978-1-84528-476-3

HEALING FOODS, HEALTHY FOODS
Using superfoods to help fight disease and maintain a healthy body

Gloria Halim

Cutting out processed and junk foods from your diet and introducing the superfoods listed in this book can help you to boost your immune system and increase your energy levels. Superfoods are rich in vitamins, minerals and anti-oxidants. This book lists them individually and explains why they are so good for you and how they can help keep you healthy. It also lists a number of spices which have medicinal benefits in their own right. By combining these spices with some of the superfoods, this book includes some simple but delicious recipes that have their roots in the Mediterranean, Asian and African regions, all of which are known for having the healthiest diets in the world.

ISBN 978-1-905862-53-5

How To Books are available through all good bookshops, or you can order direct from us through Grantham Book Services.

Tel: +44 (0)1476 541080
Fax: +44 (0)1476 541061
Email: **orders@gbs.tbs-ltd.co.uk**

Or via our website

www.howtobooks.co.uk

To order via any of these methods please quote the title(s) of the book(s) and your credit card number together with its expiry date.

For further information about our books and catalogue, please contact:

How To Books
Spring Hill House
Spring Hill Road
Begbroke
Oxford
OX5 1RX

Visit our web site at

www.howtobooks.co.uk

Or you can contact us by email at **info@howtobooks.co.uk**